KT-527-819

BRUCE SPRINGSTEEN
SONGS

BRUCE SPRINGSTEEN
SONGS

This edition published in 2003
by Virgin Books Ltd
Thames Wharf Studios
Rainville Road
London, W6 9HA

First published in the UK in 1998 by Virgin Books

Published in the USA in 1998, 2003 by Avon Books Inc.

Copyright © 1998, 2003 by Bruce Springsteen.
Song copyrights appear on page 341, which serves as an extension of this copyright

This book is sold subject to the condition that it shall not, by way of trade or otherwise, be lent, resold, hired out or otherwise circulated without the publisher's prior written consent in any form of binding or cover other than that in which it is published and without a similar condition including this condition being imposed upon the subsequent purchaser.

ISBN 0 7535 0862 1

Printed in Italy

A catalogue record for this book is available from the British Library

Project Director: Sandra Choron
Editor: Robert Santelli
Design: Sandra Choron, Harry Choron
Management: Jon Landau Management

In memory of Douglas Springsteen
1924–1998

contents

growin' up

I stood stonelike at midnight suspend-
    ed in my masquerade
I combed my hair till it was just right
    and commanded the night brigade
I was open to pain and crossed by the
    rain and I walked on a crooked
    crutch
I strolled all alone through a fallout
    zone and came out with my soul
    untouched
I hid in the clouded wrath of the crowd
    but when they said "Sit down" I
    stood up
Ooh . . . growin' up

The flag of piracy flew from my mast,
    my sails were set wing-to-wing
I had a jukebox graduate for first
    mate, she couldn't sail but she sure
    could sing
I pushed B-52 and bombed 'em with
    the blues with my gear set stubborn
    on standing
I broke all the rules, strafed my old

high school, never once gave thought
    to landing
I hid in the clouded warmth of the
    crowd but when they said "Come
    down" I threw up
Ooh . . . growin' up

I took month-long vacations in the
    stratosphere and you know it's really
    hard to hold your breath
I swear I lost everything I ever loved or
    feared, I was the cosmic kid in full
    costume dress
Well my feet they finally took root in the
    earth but I got me a nice little place
    in the stars
And I swear I found the key to the
    universe in the engine of an old
    parked car
I hid in the mother breast of the crowd
    but when they said "Pull down" I
    pulled up
Ooh . . . growin' up
Ooh . . . growin' up

mary queen of arkansas

Mary queen of Arkansas, it's not too
    early for dreamin'
The sky is grown with cloud seed sown
    and a bastard's love can be
    redeeming
Mary, my queen, your soft hulk is
    reviving
No you're not too late to desecrate, the
    servants are just rising

Well I'm just a lonely acrobat, the live
    wire is my trade
I've been a shine boy for your acid brat
    and a wharf rat of your state
Mary, my queen, your blows for freedom
    are missing
You're not man enough for me to hate or
    woman enough for kissing

The big top is for dreamers, we can take
    the circus all the way to the border
And the gallows wait for martyrs whose
    papers are in order

But I was not born to live to die and you
    were not born for queenin'
It's not too late to infiltrate, the ser-
    vants are just leavin'

Mary queen of Arkansas, your white
    skin is deceivin'
You wake and wait to lie in bait and you
    almost got me believin'
But on your bed Mary I can see the
    shadow of a noose
I don't understand how you can hold me
    so tight and love me so damn loose

But I know a place where we can go
    Mary
Where I can get a good job and start
    out all over again clean
I got contacts deep in Mexico where the
    servants have been seen

lost in the flood

The ragamuffin gunner is returnin'
   home like a hungry runaway
He walks through town all alone
"He must be from the fort" he hears the
   high school girls say
His countryside's burnin' with wolfman
   fairies dressed in drag for homicide
The hit-and-run plead sanctuary, 'neath
   a holy stone they hide
They're breakin' beams and crosses
   with a spastic's reelin' perfection
Nuns run bald through Vatican halls
   pregnant, pleadin' Immaculate
   Conception
And everybody's wrecked on Main Street
   from drinking unholy blood
Sticker smiles sweet as Gunner
   breathes deep, his ankles caked
   in mud
And I said "Hey Gunner man, that's
   quicksand, that's quicksand, that
   ain't mud
Have you thrown your senses to the war
   or did you lose them in the flood?"

That pure American brother dull-eyed
   and empty-faced

Races Sundays in Jersey in a Chevy
   stock super eight
He rides 'er low on the hip, on the side
   he's got "bound for glory" in red,
   white and blue flash paint
He leans on the hood telling racing
   stories, the kids call him Jimmy the
   Saint
Well that blaze and noise boy, he's
   gunnin' that bitch loaded to blastin'
   point
He rides head first into a hurricane and
   disappears into a point
And there's nothin' left but some blood
   where the body fell
That is, nothin' left that you could sell
Just junk all across the horizon, a real
   highwayman's farewell
And I said "Hey kid, you think that's oil?
   Man, that ain't oil, that's blood"
I wonder what he was thinking when he
   hit that storm
Or was he just lost in the flood?

Eighth Avenue sailors in satin shirts
   whisper in the air

Some storefront incarnation of Maria,
   she's puttin' on me the stare
And Bronx's best apostle stands with
   his hand on his own hardware
Everything stops, you hear five quick
   shots, the cops come up for air
And now the whiz-bang gang from
   uptown, they're shootin' up the street
And that cat from the Bronx starts
   lettin' loose
But he gets blown right off his feet
And some kid comes blastin' 'round the
   corner but a cop puts him right away
He lays on the street holding his leg
   screaming something in Spanish
Still breathing when I walked away
And someone said "Hey man, did you
   see that? His body hit the street with
   such a beautiful thud"
I wonder what the dude was sayin', or
   was he just lost in the flood?
Hey man, did you see that, those poor
   cats are sure messed up
I wonder what they were gettin' into, or
   were they all just lost in the flood?

the angel

The angel rides with hunchbacked
    children, poison oozing from his
    engine
Wieldin' love as a lethal weapon on his
    way to hubcap heaven
Baseball cards poked in his spokes, his
    boots in oil he's patiently soaked
The roadside attendant nervously jokes
    as the angel's tires stroke his
    precious pavement

The interstate's choked with nomadic
    hordes
In Volkswagen vans with full running
    boards dragging great anchors
Followin' dead-end signs into the stores
The angel rides by humpin' his hunk
    metal whore

Madison Avenue's claim to fame in a
    trainer bra with eyes like rain
She rubs against the weather-beaten
    frame and asks the angel for his
    name
Off in the distance the marble dome
Reflects across the flatlands with a
    naked feel off into parts unknown
The woman strokes his polished chrome
    and lies beside the angel's bones

for you

Princess cards she sends me with her
  regards
Barroom eyes shine vacancy, to see her
  you got to look hard
Wounded deep in battle, I stand stuffed
  like some soldier undaunted
To her Cheshire smile, I'll stand on file,
  she's all I ever wanted
But you let your blue walls get in the
  way of these facts
Honey get your carpetbaggers off my
  back
You wouldn't even give me time to cover
  my tracks
You said "Here's your mirror and your
  ball and jacks" but they're not what I
  came for and I'm sure you see that
  too
I came for you, for you, I came for you,
  but you did not need my urgency
I came for you, for you, I came for you,
  but your life was one long emergency
And your cloud line urges me and my
  electric surges free
Crawl into my ambulance, your pulse is
  getting weak
Reveal yourself all now to me girl while
  you've got the strength to speak
'Cause they're waiting for you at
  Bellevue with their oxygen masks
But I could give it all to you now if only
  you could ask

And don't call for your surgeon, even he
  says it's too late
It's not your lungs this time, it's your
  heart that holds your fate
Don't give me my money honey I don't
  want it back
You and your pony face and your union
  jack
Well take your local joker and teach him
  how to act
I swear I was never that way even when
  I really cracked
Didn't you think I knew that you were
  born with the power of a locomotive
Able to leap tall buildings in a single
  bound
And your Chelsea suicide with no
  apparent motive
You could laugh and cry in a single
  sound

And your strength is devastating in the
  face of all these odds
Remember how I kept you waiting when
  it was my turn to be the god

You were not quite half so proud when I
  found you broken on the beach
Remember how I poured salt on your
  tongue and hung just out of reach
And the band they played the homecoming theme as I caressed your
  cheek
That ragged jagged melody she still
  clings to me like a leech
But that medal you wore on your chest
  always got in the way
Like a little girl with a trophy so soft to
  buy her way
We were both hitchhikers but you had
  your ear tuned to the roar
Of some metal-tempered engine on an
  alien distant shore
So you left to find a better reason than
  the one we were living for
And it's not that nursery mouth I came
  back for
And it's not the way you're stretched out
  on the floor
'Cause I've broken all your windows and
  I've rammed through all your doors
And who am I to ask you to lick my
  sores
And you should know that's true
I came for you, for you, I came for you,
  but you did not need my urgency
I came for you, for you, I came for you,
  but your life was one long emergency
And your cloud line urges me and my
  electric surges free

spirit in the night

Crazy Janey and her mission man were
back in the alley tradin' hands
'Long came Wild Billy with his friend
G-man all duded up for Saturday
night
Well Billy slammed on his coaster
brakes and said anybody wanna go
up to Greasy Lake
It's about a mile down on the dark side
of Route 88
I got a bottle of rosé so let's try it
We'll pick up Hazy Davy and Killer Joe
and I'll take you all out to where the
gypsy angels go
They're built like light
And they dance like spirits in the night
(all night) in the night (all night)
Oh you don't know what they can do
to you
Spirits in the night (all night) in the
night (all night)
Stand right up now and let them shoot
through you

Well now Wild Billy was a crazy cat and
he shook some dust out of his coon-
skin cap
He said "Trust some of this it'll show
you where you're at or at least it'll
help you really feel it"
By the time we made it up to Greasy
Lake I had my head out the window
and Janey's fingers were in the cake
I think I really dug her 'cause I was too
loose to fake

I said "I'm hurt," she said "Honey let
me heal it"
And we danced all night to a soul fairy
band
And she kissed me just right like only a
lonely angel can
She felt so nice, just as soft as a spirit
in the night (all night) in the night
(all night)
Janey don't know what she do to you
Like a spirit in the night (all night) in
the night (all night)
Stand right up and let it shoot through
me

Now the night was bright and the stars
threw light on Billy and Davy dancin'
in the moonlight
They were down near the water in a
stoned mud fight
Killer Joe gone passed out on the lawn
Well now Hazy Davy got really hurt, he
ran into the lake in just his socks
and a shirt
Me and Crazy Janey was makin' love in
the dirt singin' our birthday songs
Janey said it was time to go so we
closed our eyes and said good-bye to
gypsy angel row, felt so right
Together we moved like spirits in the
night (all night) in the night (all
night)

14 →14A →15 →15A →16 →16A
KODAK SAFETY FILM

it's hard to be a saint in the city

I had skin like leather and the
diamond-hard look of a cobra
I was born blue and weathered but I
burst just like a supernova
I could walk like Brando right into
the sun
Then dance just like a Casanova
With my blackjack and jacket and hair
slicked sweet
Silver star studs on my duds just like a
Harley in heat
When I strut down the street I could feel
its heartbeat
The sisters fell back and said "Don't
that man look pretty"
The cripple on the corner cried out
"Nickels for your pity"
Them gasoline boys downtown sure talk
gritty
It's so hard to be a saint in the city

I was the king of the alley, mama I
could talk some trash
I was the prince of the paupers crowned
downtown at the beggar's bash
I was the pimp's main prophet, I kept
everything cool
Just a backstreet gambler with the luck
to lose
And when the heat came down and it
was left on the ground
The devil appeared like Jesus through
the steam in the street
Showin' me a hand I knew even the
cops couldn't beat
I felt his hot breath on my neck as I
dove into the heat
It's so hard to be a saint when you're
just a boy out on the street

And the sages of the subway sit just
like the living dead

As the tracks clack out the rhythm,
their eyes fixed straight ahead
They ride the line of balance and hold
on by just a thread
But it's too hot in these tunnels, you
can get hit up by the heat
You get up to get out at your next stop
but they push you back down in
your seat
Your heart starts beatin' faster as you
struggle to your feet
Then you're out of that hole and back
up on the street

And them Southside sisters sure look
pretty
The cripple on the corner cries out
"Nickels for your pity"
And them downtown boys sure talk
gritty
It's so hard to be a saint in the city

4th of july, asbury park [sandy]

Sandy, the fireworks are hailin' over
Little Eden tonight
Forcin' a light into all those stoney
faces left stranded on this warm July
Down in town the circuit's full with
switchblade lovers so fast, so shiny,
so sharp
As the wizards play down on Pinball
Way on the boardwalk way past dark
And the boys from the casino dance
with their shirts open like Latin
lovers on the shore
Chasin' all them silly New York virgins
by the score

Sandy, the aurora is risin' behind us
This pier lights our carnival life
forever
Love me tonight for I may never see you
again
Hey Sandy girl, my baby

Now the greasers they tramp the streets
or get busted for sleeping on the
beach all night
Them boys in their high heels, ah
Sandy, their skins are so white
And me I just got tired of hangin' in
them dusty arcades bangin' them
pleasure machines
Chasin' the factory girls underneath the
boardwalk where they promise to
unsnap their jeans
And you know that tilt-a-whirl down on
the south beach drag
I got on it last night and my shirt got
caught
And they kept me spinnin'
I didn't think I'd ever get off

Oh Sandy, the aurora is risin' behind us
This pier lights our carnival life on the
water
Runnin', laughin' 'neath the boardwalk
with the boss's daughter
I remember, Sandy girl, now baby

Sandy, that waitress I was seeing lost
her desire for me
I spoke with her last night, she said
she won't set herself on fire for me
anymore
She worked that joint under the boardwalk, she was always the girl you
saw boppin' down the beach with the
radio
The kids say last night she was dressed
like a star in one of them cheap little
seaside bars and I saw her parked
with Loverboy out on the Kokomo
Did you hear the cops finally busted
Madam Marie for tellin' fortunes
better than they do
For me this boardwalk life is through
You ought to quit this scene too

Sandy, the aurora is rising behind us
This pier lights our carnival life
forever
Oh love me tonight and I promise I'll
love you forever

kitty's back

Catlong sighs holding Kitty's black
   tooth
She left to marry some top cat, ain't it
   the cold truth
And there hasn't been a tally since
   Sally left the alley
Since Kitty left with Big Pretty things
   have got pretty thin
It's tight on this fence since them
   young dudes are musclin' in

Jack Knife cries 'cause baby's in a
   bundle
She goes running nightly, lightly
   through the jungle
And them tin cans are explodin' out in
   the ninety-degree heat
Cat somehow lost his baby down on
   Bleecker Street
It's sad but it sure is true
Cat shrugs his shoulders, sits back and
   sighs
Ooh, what can I do, ooh, what can I do?
Ooh, what can I do, ooh, what can I do?

Catlong lies back bent on a trash can
Flashing lights cut the night, dude in
   white says he's the man

Well you better learn to move fast when
   you're young or you're not long
   around
Cat somehow lost his Kitty down in the
   city pound
So get right, get tight, get down
Well who's that down at the end of the
   alley?
She's been gone so long

Kitty's back in town, here she comes
   now
Kitty's back in town
Kitty's back in town, here she comes
   now
Kitty's back in town
Kitty's back in town, here she comes
   now
Kitty's back in town

Now Cat knows his Kitty's been untrue
And that she left him for a city dude
But she's so soft, she's so blue
When he looks into her eyes
He just sits back and sighs
Ooh, what can I do, ooh, what can I do?

wild billy's circus story

The machinist climbs his ferris wheel
  like a brave
And the fire eater's lyin' in a pool of
  sweat, victim of the heatwave
Behind the tent the hired hand tightens
  his legs on the sword swallower's
  blade
And circus town's on the shortwave

The runway lies ahead like a great false
  dawn
Fat lady, big mama, Missy Bimbo sits
  in her chair and yawns
And the man-beast lies in his cage
  sniffin' popcorn
As the midget licks his fingers and
  suffers Missy Bimbo's scorn
Circus town's been born

Whoa, and a press roll drummer go
  ballerina to and fro
Cartwheelin' up on that tightrope with
  a cannon blast lightnin' flash
Movin' fast through the tent Mars bent,
  he's gonna miss his fall
Oh God save the human cannonball
And the flying Zambinis watch
  Margarita do her neck twist
And the ringmaster gets the crowd to
  count along: "Ninety-five, ninety-six,
  ninety-seven"
A ragged suitcase in his hand, he

steals silently away from the circus
  grounds
And the highway's haunted by the
  carnival sounds
They dance like a great greasepaint
  ghost on the wind
A man in baggy pants, a lonely face, a
  crazy grin
Runnin' home to some small Ohio town
Jesus send some good women to save
  all your clowns

And circus boy dances like a monkey on
  barbed wire
And the barker romances with a junkie,
  she's got a flat tire
And now the elephants dance real funky
  and the band plays like a jungle fire
Circus town's on the live wire
And the strong man Sampson lifts the
  midget Little Tiny Tim way up on his
  shoulders, way up
And carries him on down the midway
  past the kids, past the sailors
To his dimly lit trailer
And the ferris wheel turns and turns
  like it ain't ever gonna stop
And the circus boss leans over,
  whispers in the little boy's ear "Hey
  son, you wanna try the big top?"
All aboard, Nebraska's our next stop

incident on 57th street

Spanish Johnny drove in from the
   underworld last night
With bruised arms and broken rhythm
   in a beat-up old Buick
But dressed just like dynamite
He tried sellin' his heart to the hard
   girls over on Easy Street
But they sighed "Johnny it falls apart
   so easy and you know hearts these
   days are cheap"
And the pimps swung their axes and
   said "Johnny you're a cheater"
Well the pimps swung their axes and
   said "Johnny you're a liar"
And from out of the shadows came
   a young girl's voice said "Johnny
   don't cry"
Puerto Rican Jane, oh won't you tell me
   what's your name
I want to drive you down to the other
   side of town where paradise ain't so
   crowded, there'll be action goin'
   down on Shanty Lane tonight
All them golden-heeled fairies in a real
   bitch fight
Pull .38s and kiss the girls good night
Oh good night, it's all right Jane
Now let them black boys in to light the
   soul flame

We may find it out on the street tonight
   baby
Or we may walk until the daylight
   maybe

Well like a cool Romeo he made his
   moves, oh she looked so fine
Like a late Juliet she knew he'd never
   be true but then she didn't really
   mind
Upstairs a band was playin', the singer
   was singin' something about goin'
   home
She whispered "Spanish Johnny, you
   can leave me tonight but just don't
   leave me alone"

And Johnny cried "Puerto Rican Jane,
   word is down the cops have found
   the vein"
Oh them barefoot boys they left their
   homes for the woods
Them little barefoot street boys they
   say homes ain't no good
They left the corners, threw away all
   their switchblade knives and kissed
   each other good-bye

Johnny was sittin' on the fire escape

watchin' the kids playin' down the
   street
He called down "Hey little heroes,
   summer's long but I guess it ain't
   very sweet around here anymore"
Janey sleeps in sheets damp with
   sweat, Johnny sits up alone and
   watches her dream on, dream on
And the sister prays for lost souls, then
   breaks down in the chapel after
   everyone's gone

Jane moves over to share her pillow but
   opens her eyes to see Johnny up and
   puttin' his clothes on
She says "Those romantic young boys
All they ever want to do is fight"
Those romantic young boys
They're callin' through the window
"Hey Spanish Johnny, you want to make
   a little easy money tonight?"
And Johnny whispered:
Good night, it's all tight Jane
I'll meet you tomorrow night on Lover's
   Lane
We may find it out on the street tonight
   baby
Or we may walk until the daylight
   maybe

rosalita [come out tonight]

Spread out now Rosie, doctor come cut
   loose her mama's reins
You know playin' blindman's bluff is a
   little baby's game
You pick up Little Dynamite, I'm gonna
   pick up Little Gun
And together we're gonna go out
   tonight and make that highway run
You don't have to call me lieutenant
   Rosie and I don't want to be your son
The only lover I'm ever gonna need's
   your soft sweet little girl's tongue
Rosie you're the one
Dynamite's in the belfry playin' with the
   bats
Little Gun's downtown in front of
   Woolworth's tryin' out his attitude on
   all the cats
Papa's on the corner waitin' for the bus
Mama she's home in the window waitin'
   up for us
She'll be there in that chair when they
   wrestle her upstairs
'Cause you know we ain't gonna come
I ain't here on business
I'm only here for fun
And Rosie you're the one

CHORUS:
Rosalita jump a little lighter
Señorita come sit by my fire

I just want to be your love, ain't no lie
Rosalita you're my stone desire

Jack the Rabbit and Weak Knees Willie,
   you know they're gonna be there
Ah, Sloppy Sue and Big Bones Billy,
   they'll be comin' up for air
We're gonna play some pool, skip some
   school, act real cool
Stay out all night, it's gonna feel all
   right
So Rosie come out tonight, baby come
   out tonight
Windows are for cheaters, chimneys for
   the poor
Closets are for hangers, winners use
   the door
So use it, Rosie, that's what it's there
   for

(CHORUS)

Now I know your mama she don't like
   me 'cause I play in a rock and roll
   band
And I know your daddy he don't dig me
   but he never did understand
Papa lowered the boom, he locked you
   in your room
I'm comin' to lend a hand
I'm comin' to liberate you, confiscate

you, I want to be your man
Someday we'll look back on this and it
   will all seem funny
But now you're sad, your mama's mad
And your papa says he knows that I
   don't have any money
Tell him this is his last chance to get
   his daughter in a fine romance
Because the record company, Rosie,
   just gave me a big advance

My tires were slashed and I almost
   crashed but the Lord had mercy
My machine she's a dud, I'm stuck in
   the mud somewhere in the swamps
   of Jersey
Hold on tight, stay up all night 'cause
   Rosie I'm comin' on strong
By the time we meet the morning light I
   will hold you in my arms
I know a pretty little place in Southern
   California down San Diego way
There's a little café where they play
   guitars all night and all day
You can hear them in the back room
   strummin'
So hold tight baby 'cause don't you
   know daddy's comin'

(CHORUS)

new york city serenade

Billy he's down by the railroad track
Sittin' low in the backseat of his
    Cadillac
Diamond Jackie, she's so intact
As she falls so softly beneath him
Jackie's heels are stacked
Billy's got cleats on his boots
Together they're gonna boogaloo down
    Broadway and come back home with
    the loot
It's midnight in Manhattan, this is no
    time to get cute
It's a mad dog's promenade
So walk tall or baby don't walk at all

Fish lady, oh fish lady
She baits them tenement walls
She won't take corner boys
They ain't got no money
And they're so easy
I said "Hey, baby
Won't you take my hand
Walk with me down Broadway
Well mama take my arm and move with
    me down Broadway"
I'm a young man, I talk it real loud
Yeah babe I walk it real proud for you
Ah, so shake it away
So shake away your street life
Shake away your city life
Hook up to the train
And hook up to the night train
Hook it up

Hook up to the train
But I know she won't take the train, no
    sho won't take the train
Oh she won't take the train, no she
    won't take the train
Oh she won't take the train, no she
    won't take the train
Oh she won't take the train, no she
    won't take the train
She's afraid them tracks are gonna slow
    her down
And when she turns this boy'll be gone
So long, sometimes you just gotta
    walk on, walk on

Hey vibes man, hey jazz man, play me
    your serenade
Any deeper blue and you'd be playin' in
    your grave
Save your notes, don't spend 'em on the
    blues boy
Save your notes, don't spend 'em on
    the darlin' yearling sharp boy
Straight for the church note ringin',
    vibes man sting a trash can
Listen to your junk man
Listen to your junk man
Listen to your junk man
He's singin', he's singin', he's singin'
All dressed up in satin, walkin' down
    the alley
He's singin', singin', singin', singin'

born to run

n 1974, though struggling through the aftermath of the riots and economic depression, Asbury Park still managed to come to life on Friday and Saturday nights. Down by the boardwalk, Kingsley and Ocean avenues formed a sort of racetrack oval that locals called the Circuit. It surrounded all the bars and nightclubs, including the Stone Pony, the new hub of the city's rock music scene.

In '70s New Jersey, the car was still a powerful image. That summer I bought my first set of wheels for two thousand dollars. It was a '57 Chevy with dual, four-barrel carbs, a Hurst on the floor, and orange flames spread across the hood. I was living in a small house in West Long Branch, up the coast from Asbury. I had a record player by the side of my bed. At night I'd lie back and listen to records by Roy Orbison, the Ronettes, the Beach Boys, and other great '60s artists. These were records whose full depth I'd missed the first time around. But now I was appreciating their craft and power.

One day I was playing my guitar on the edge of my bed, working on some song ideas, and the words "born to run" came into my head. At first I thought it was the name of a movie or something I'd seen on a car spinning around the Circuit, but I couldn't be certain. I liked the phrase because it suggested a cinematic drama I thought would work with the music I was hearing in my head.

Before we had a chance to record it, "Born to Run" developed as a song that the E Street Band and I played live on the road. That gave me an opportunity to feel out the arrangement. But live, the limitations of a seven-piece band were never going to provide me with the range of sound I needed to realize the song's potential. It was the first piece of music I wrote and conceived as a studio production. It was connected to the long, live pieces I'd written previously by the twists and turns of the arrangement.

But "Born to Run" was more condensed; it maintained the excitement of "Rosalita" while delivering its message in less time and with a shorter burst of energy. This was a turning point, and it allowed me to open up my music to a far larger audience. "Born to Run" was a long time coming; it took me six months to write. But it proved to be the key to my songwriting for the rest of the record. Lyrically, I was entrenched in classic rock and roll images, and I wanted to find a way to use those images without their feeling anachronistic.

Born to Run was released into post-Vietnam America. There was a coming gas crisis . . . no gas . . . no cars. People were contemplating a country that was finite, where resources and life had lim-

The Jabongans (a.k.a. the E Street Band) with new members Max Weinberg *(third from right)* and Roy Bittan *(far right)*

With Jon Landau

its. Slowly, the dread that I managed to keep out of "Rosalita" squeezed its way into the lives of the people on *Born to Run*.

It was during this time that I began my friendship with Jon Landau, a Boston music writer. I sent him a tape of *Born to Run* while he was in the hospital recuperating from an illness. He later moved to New York City. There we struck up a relationship—hanging out, talking music, and listening to records. When I ran into trouble recording the rest of the album, he stepped in and helped me get the job done. We moved into the Record Plant in New York City and hired Jimmy Iovine to engineer. We stripped down the songs and streamlined the arrangements. We developed a more direct sound with cleaner lines.

"Thunder Road" opens the album, introducing its characters and its central proposition: Do you want to take a chance? On us? On life? You're then led through the band bio and block party of "Tenth Avenue Freeze-out," the broken friendships of "Backstreets," out into the open with "Born to Run," and into the dark city and spiritual battleground of "Jungleland."

Few of the album's songs were written on guitar. The orchestral sound of *Born to Run* came from most of the songs being written on piano. It was on the keyboard that I could find the arrangements needed to accompany the stories I was writing. "Born to Run," which began on the guitar with the riff that opens the song, was finished on the piano.

The characters on *Born to Run* were less eccentric and less local than on *Greetings* and *The Wild, the Innocent.* They could have been anybody and everybody. When the screen door slams on "Thunder Road," you're not necessarily on the Jersey Shore anymore. You could be anywhere in America. These were the beginnings of the characters whose lives I would trace in my work for the next two decades.

As a songwriter I always felt one of my jobs was to face the questions that evolve out of my music and search for the answers as best as I could. For me, the primary questions I'd be writing about for the rest of my work life first took form in the songs on *Born to Run* ("I want to know if love is real."). It was the album where I left behind my adolescent definitions of love and freedom.

Born to Run was the dividing line.

born to run

In the day we sweat it out on the
streets of a runaway American dream
At night we ride through mansions of
glory in suicide machines
Sprung from cages on Highway 9
Chrome-wheeled fuel-injected
And steppin' out over the line
Baby this town rips the bones from your
back
It's a death trap, it's a suicide rap
We gotta get out while we're young
'Cause tramps like us, baby we were
born to run

Wendy let me in, I wanna be your friend
I want to guard your dreams and
visions
Just wrap your legs 'round these velvet
rims
And strap your hands across my
engines

Together we could break this trap
We'll run till we drop, baby we'll never
go back
Will you walk with me out on the wire
'Cause baby I'm just a scared and
lonely rider
But I gotta know how it feels
I want to know if your love is wild
Girl I want to know if love is real

Beyond the Palace hemipowered drones
scream down the boulevard
The girls comb their hair in rearview
mirrors
And the boys try to look so hard
The amusement park rises bold and
stark
Kids are huddled on the beach in the
mist
I wanna die with you out on the streets
tonight

In an everlasting kiss

The highway's jammed with broken
heroes
On a last chance power drive
Everybody's out on the run tonight
But there's no place left to hide
Together, Wendy, we can live with the
sadness
I'll love you with all the madness in my
soul
Someday girl, I don't know when, we're
gonna get to that place
Where we really want to go
And we'll walk in the sun
But till then tramps like us
Baby we were born to run

she's the one

With her killer graces
And her secret places
That no boy can fill
With her hands on her hips
Oh and that smile on her lips
Because she knows that it kills me
With her soft French cream
Standing in that doorway like a dream
I wish she'd just leave me alone
Because French cream won't soften
   them boots
And French kisses will not break that
   heart of stone
With her long hair falling
And her eyes that shine like a midnight
   sun
Oh she's the one
She's the one

That thunder in your heart
At night when you're kneeling in the
   dark
It says you're never gonna leave her
But there's this angel in her eyes
That tells such desperate lies

And all you want to do is believe her
And tonight you'll try
Just one more time
To leave it all behind
And to break on through
Oh she can take you
But if she wants to break you
She's gonna find out that ain't so easy
   to do
And no matter where you sleep
Tonight or how far you run
Oh she's the one
She's the one

Oh and just one kiss
She'd fill them long summer nights
With her tenderness
That secret pact you made
Back when her love could save you
From the bitterness
Oh she's the one
Oh she's the one
Oh she's the one
Oh she's the one

meeting across the river

Hey Eddie, can you lend me a few bucks
And tonight can you get us a ride?
Gotta make it through the tunnel
Got a meeting with a man on the other
   side

Hey Eddie, this guy he's the real thing
So if you want to come along
You gotta promise you won't say
   anything
'Cause this guy don't dance
And the word's been passed this is our
   last chance

We gotta stay cool tonight, Eddie
'Cause man, we got ourselves out on
   that line
And if we blow this one
They ain't gonna be looking for just me
   this time
And all we gotta do is hold up our end

Here stuff this in your pocket
It'll look like you're carrying a friend
And remember, just don't smile
Change your shirt 'cause tonight we
   got style

Well Cherry says she's gonna walk
'Cause she found out I took her radio
   and hocked it
But Eddie, man, she don't understand
That two grand's practically sitting here
   in my pocket
And tonight's gonna be everything that
   I said
And when I walk through that door
I'm just gonna throw that money on the
   bed
She'll see this time I wasn't just talking
Then I'm gonna go out walking

Hey Eddie, can you catch us a ride?

Worksheet for "Meeting Across the River"

Hey Eddie can you lend me a few bucks
    And tonight can you get us a ride
gotta make it through the tunnel gotta
    meetin' with a man on the other side
And Eddie this guys he's the real
    thing so if you wanna come allong
you gotta promise you won't say anythin
cause this guy don't dance and doin
~~you know this is cor~~ the words passed
        this our last chance

We gotta stay
        ~~too~~ cool tonight Eddie man we got
oursevles the rep on the line
    And if we ~~blow~~ lose this one they ain't
gonna be looking for just me this time
    All we gotta do is hold up our end
here stuff this in your pocker it'll look
like your carryin a freind remember
    don't smile change your shirt tonight
were goin in style

    Cherry says she's gonna walk cause
I took the radio and hocked it
but man she don't understand that
two grands practically in my pocker
tonight so gonna be everything I
said and when I walk through
that door I'm gonna throw that
money on the bed she'll see this time
I wasn't just talkin then I'm gonna
    go out walkin

Following a seventy-two-hour studio marathon, *Born to Run* was completed. At 8:30 A.M. the band rehearsed to begin the tour in Providence, Rhode Island, that night.

jungleland

The Rangers had a homecoming
In Harlem late last night
And the Magic Rat drove his sleek
machino
Over the Jersey state line
Barefoot girl sitting on the hood of a
Dodge
Drinking warm beer in the soft summer
rain
The Rat pulls into town, rolls up his
pants
Together they take a stab at romance
And disappear down Flamingo Lane

Well the Maximum Lawmen run down
Flamingo
Chasing the Rat and the barefoot girl
And the kids 'round there live just like
shadows
Always quiet, holding hands
From the churches to the jails
Tonight all is silence in the world
As we take our stand
Down in Jungleland

The midnight gang's assembled
And picked a rendezvous for the night
They'll meet 'neath that giant Exxon
sign

That brings this fair city light
Man there's an opera out on the
turnpike
There's a ballet being fought out in
the alley
Until the local cops
Cherry tops
Rips this holy night
The street's alive
As secret debts are paid
Contacts made, they vanish unseen
Kids flash guitars just like switch-
blades
Hustling for the record machine
The hungry and the hunted
Explode into rock and roll bands
That face off against each other out in
the street
Down in Jungleland

In the parking lot the visionaries
Dress in the latest rage
Inside the backstreet girls are dancing
To the records that the DJ plays
Lonely-hearted lovers
Struggle in dark corners
Desperate as the night moves on
Just one look and a whisper
And they're gone

Beneath the city two hearts beat
Soul engines running through a night
so tender
In a bedroom locked
In whispers of soft refusal
And then surrender
In the tunnels uptown
The Rat's own dream guns him down
As shots echo down them hallways in
the night
No one watches when the ambulance
pulls away
Or as the girl shuts out the bedroom
light

Outside the street's on fire
In a real death waltz
Between what's flesh and what's
fantasy
And the poets down here
Don't write nothing at all
They just stand back and let it all be
And in the quick of a knife
They reach for their moment
And try to make an honest stand
But they wind up wounded
Not even dead
Tonight in Jungleland

darkness
on the
edge
of town

fter *Born to Run* I wanted to write about life in the close confines of the small towns I grew up in. In 1977 I was living on a farm in Holmdel, New Jersey. It was there that I wrote most of the songs for *Darkness on the Edge of Town*.

I was twenty-seven and the product of Top 40 radio. Songs like the Animals' "It's My Life" and "We Gotta Get Out of This Place" were infused with an early pop class consciousness. That, along with my own experience—the stress and tension of my father's and mother's life that came with the difficulties of trying to make ends meet—influenced my writing. I had a reaction to my own good fortune. I asked myself new questions. I felt a sense of account-ability to the people I'd grown up alongside of. I began to wonder how to address that feeling. Also,

With Chuck Plotkin, Jon Landau, and engineer Jimmy Iovine

wanted my new characters to feel weathered, older, but not beaten. The sense of daily struggle in each song greatly increased. The possibility of transcendence or any sort of personal redemption felt a lot harder to come by. This was the tone I wanted to sustain. I intentionally steered away from any hint of escapism and set my characters down in the middle of a community under siege. Weeks, even months went by, before I had something that felt right.

The songs came together slowly, line by line, piece by piece. The titles were big: "Adam Raised a Cain," "Darkness on the Edge of Town," "Racing in the Street." "Adam Raised a Cain" used biblical images to summon up the love and bitterness between a father and son. "Darkness on the Edge of Town" dealt with the idea that the setting for personal transformation is often found at the end of your rope. In "Racing in the Street" I wanted my street racers to carry the years between the car songs of the '60s and 1978 America. To make "Racing" and those other big titles personal, I had to infuse the music with my own hopes and fears. If you don't do that, your characters ring hollow, and you're left with rhetoric, words without meaning.

Most of my writing is emotionally autobiographical. You've got pull up the things that mean something to you in order for them to mean anything to your audience. That's how they know you're not kidding.

With the record's final verse, "Tonight I'll be on that hill . . . ," my characters stand unsure of their fate, but dug in and committed. By the end of *Darkness* I'd found my adult voice.

A long time ago we chose to ride *or* die

Hot Rod Storys   Breakers Point
The Hot Rod Story   Breakout
                         The Wait

          Prove it All Night
I Believe in a Promised Land
          Fury/Let the Quiet Rain Fall
    Initiations /   the Ride
          Thunder Road /
Kingsley Avenue
                         Ho
    The Searchers
              the
Workin
              the Taker
Collision /
          Factory / Tarni

          Fa

Titles
          2 - try brighter sound
          3 - best
          4 - good
          5 - vocal too loud

Angels on Wheels / American Relay
Demolition Derby   Hot Rod Angels
Speed Racing through America
          (Int)
Racin in the Street / Buried Crosses
                         Medals
          Speed Racing in America
I Ride the Serpent / Grace / National
          Daytona Screamer
Ramrod / Kansas City Confidential
          Street Racer
Ramrodin
              Faded Medals
    Dirt Tracker
                    Badlands
Daytona
          Gun Crazy / Bear Town
Who Walk in Darkness   Ignition
Monroe County Line / Go
Waynesboro   Something in the
County   Night

Often I'd work from pages of titles I collected
as I went along.

badlands

Lights out tonight
Trouble in the heartland
Got a head-on collision
Smashin' in my guts, man
I'm caught in a crossfire
That I don't understand
But there's one thing I know for sure,
  girl
I don't give a damn
For the same old played out scenes
I don't give a damn
For just the in-betweens
Honey, I want the heart, I want the soul
I want control right now
You better listen to me, baby
Talk about a dream
Try to make it real
You wake up in the night
With a fear so real
You spend your life waiting
For a moment that just won't come
Well don't waste your time waiting

CHORUS:
Badlands, you gotta live it every day
Let the broken hearts stand
As the price you've gotta pay
We'll keep pushin' till it's understood
And these badlands start treating us
  good

Workin' in the fields
Till you get your back burned
Workin' 'neath the wheel
Till you get your facts learned
Baby, I got my facts
Learned real good right now
You better get it straight, darlin'
Poor man wanna be rich
Rich man wanna be king
And a king ain't satisfied
Till he rules everything
I wanna go out tonight
I wanna find out what I got

I believe in the love that you gave me
I believe in the faith that can save me
I believe in the hope and I pray
That someday it may raise me
Above these badlands

(CHORUS)

For the ones who had a notion
A notion deep inside
That it ain't no sin to be glad you're
  alive
I wanna find one face that ain't looking
  through me
I wanna find one place
I wanna spit in the face of these
  badlands

(CHORUS)

adam raised
a cain

In the summer that I was baptized
My father held me to his side
As they put me to the water
He said how on that day I cried
We were prisoners of love, a love in
    chains
He was standin' in the door, I was
    standin' in the rain
With the same hot blood burning in our
    veins
Adam raised a Cain

All of the old faces
Ask you why you're back
They fit you with position
And the keys to your daddy's Cadillac
In the darkness of your room
Your mother calls you by your true name
You remember the faces, the places,
    the names

You know it's never over, it's relentless
    as the rain
Adam raised a Cain

In the Bible Cain slew Abel
And east of Eden he was cast
You're born into this life paying
For the sins of somebody else's past
Daddy worked his whole life for nothing
    but the pain
Now he walks these empty rooms
    looking for something to blame
You inherit the sins, you inherit the
    flames
Adam raised a Cain
Lost but not forgotten
From the dark heart of a dream
Adam raised a Cain

something in the night

I'm riding down Kingsley
Figuring I'll get a drink
Turn the radio up loud
So I don't have to think
I take her to the floor
Looking for a moment when the world
    seems right
And I tear into the guts
Of something in the night

You're born with nothing
And better off that way
Soon as you've got something
They send someone to try and take it
    away
You can ride this road till dawn
Without another human being in sight
Just kids wasted on
Something in the night

Nothing is forgotten or forgiven
When it's your last time around
I got stuff running 'round my head
That I just can't live down

When we found the things we loved
They were crushed and dying in the dirt
We tried to pick up the pieces
And get away without getting hurt
But they caught us at the state line
And burned our cars in one last fight
And left us running burned and blind
Chasing something in the night

candy's room

In Candy's room there are pictures of
  her heroes on the wall
But to get to Candy's room you gotta
  walk the darkness of Candy's hall
Strangers from the city call my baby's
  number and they bring her toys
When I come knocking she smiles pretty
She knows I wanna be Candy's boy
There's a sadness hidden in that pretty
  face
A sadness all her own from which no
  man can keep Candy safe

We kiss, my heart's pumpin' to my brain
The blood rushes in my veins when I
  touch Candy's lips
We go driving, driving deep into the
  night
I go driving deep into the light in
  Candy's eyes

She says baby if you wanna be wild

You got a lot to learn, close your eyes
Let them melt, let them fire
Let them burn
'Cause in the darkness there'll be
  hidden worlds that shine
When I hold Candy close she makes the
  hidden worlds mine

She has fancy clothes and diamond
  rings
She has men who give her anything she
  wants but they don't see
That what she wants is me

Oh and I want her so
I'll never let her go, no no no
She knows that I'd give
All that I've got to give
All that I want, all that I live
To make Candy mine
Tonight

New Fast Song (Candy)

In Candys room sb has pictures of her saviour / hangs
on the wall but to get to Candys room
you gotta walk Candys hall

        so rangers fum the city call my babys number
hey bring her toys but when I come knockin she
        smiles pretty she knows I'm gonna be Candys
                boy

                        braveness
here, somewhere in the darkness I find hidden worlds
(strange new worlds) that shine thru the (anger)
fear   braveness   mist
                blackness

                Then
+ when we kiss my heads comes pushin/slashin thru   explodes
                my skin   with I see myself   I break thru
        for a moment she tells me in
post a while/awhile/for many days   thats when the sadness begins   mad
        I get visions (glimpses) (dreams) of avenging angels of eden   that awakens
        with them white horse + flaming swords
                can blow this whole town into the sea
        but they cant Buth Candy + me
                our love they cannot destroy
I will forever be Candys boy

        she says baby if you wanna be wild you gotta
                you got fear - these some things   yormgs   you got a lot to learn
some   spreadout   openup go
        you gotta let your (wings) heart burn
                so come with me + together (we) baby well draw all
will go   driven together into the night   night
                thru the heart of a fire fight into no rain
region
        we go driven south thru stops   to outwards
                thru spider off the line + there we kiss

                from a world well meet / burn / take / know /
withcut end

racing in the street

I got a '69 Chevy with a 396
Fuelie heads and a Hurst on the floor
She's waiting tonight down in the
  parking lot
Outside the 7-11 store
Me and my partner Sonny built her
  straight out of scratch
And he rides with me from town to town
We only run for the money, got no
  strings attached
We shut 'em up and then we shut 'em
  down

Tonight, tonight the strip's just right
I wanna blow 'em off in my first heat
Summer's here and the time is right
For racin' in the street

We take all the action we can meet
And we cover all the northeast states
When the strip shuts down we run 'em
  in the street

From the fire roads to the interstate
Some guys they just give up living
And start dying little by little, piece by
  piece
Some guys come home from work and
  wash up
And go racin' in the street

Tonight, tonight the strip's just right
I wanna blow 'em all out of their seats
Calling out around the world, we're
  going racin' in the street

I met her on the strip three years ago
In a Camaro with this dude from L.A.
I blew that Camaro off my back
And drove that little girl away
But now there's wrinkles around my
  baby's eyes
And she cries herself to sleep at night
When I come home the house is dark

She sighs "Baby did you make it all
  right?"
She sits on the porch of her daddy's
  house
But all her pretty dreams are torn
She stares off alone into the night
With the eyes of one who hates for just
  being born
For all the shut-down strangers and
  hot-rod angels
Rumbling through this promised land
Tonight my baby and me we're gonna
  ride to the sea
And wash these sins off our hands

Tonight, tonight the highway's bright
Out of our way mister you best keep
'Cause summer's here and the time is
  right
For racin' in the street

the promised land

On a rattlesnake speedway in the Utah
   desert
I pick up my money and head back into
   town
Driving 'cross the Waynesboro county
   line
I got the radio on and I'm just killing
   time
Working all day in my daddy's garage
Driving all night chasing some mirage
Pretty soon, little girl, I'm gonna take
   charge

CHORUS:
The dogs on Main Street howl
'Cause they understand
If I could take one moment into my
   hands
Mister, I ain't a boy, no I'm a man
And I believe in a promised land

I've done my best to live the right way
I get up every morning and go to work
   each day
But your eyes go blind and your blood
   runs cold

Sometimes I feel so weak I just want to
   explode
Explode and tear this whole town apart
Take a knife and cut this pain from my
   heart
Find somebody itching for something to
   start

(CHORUS)

There's a dark cloud rising from the
   desert floor
I packed my bags and I'm heading
   straight into the storm
Gonna be a twister to blow everything
   down
That ain't got the faith to stand its
   ground
Blow away the dreams that tear you
   apart
Blow away the dreams that break your
   heart
Blow away the lies that leave you nothing but lost and brokenhearted

(CHORUS)

factory

Early in the morning factory whistle
   blows
Man rises from bed and puts on his
   clothes
Man takes his lunch, walks out in the
   morning light
It's the working, the working, just the
   working life

Through the mansions of fear, through
   the mansions of pain
I see my daddy walking through the
   factory gates in the rain
Factory takes his hearing, factory gives
   him life
The working, the working, just the
   working life

End of the day, factory whistle cries
Men walk through these gates with
   death in their eyes
And you just better believe, boy
Somebody's gonna get hurt tonight
It's the working, the working, just the
   working life

streets of fire

When the night's quiet and you don't
  care anymore
And your eyes are tired and there's
  someone at your door
And you realize you wanna let go
And the weak lies and the cold walls
  you embrace
Eat at your insides and leave you face
  to face with
Streets of fire

I'm wandering, a loser down these
  tracks
I'm dying but girl I can't go back
'Cause in the darkness I hear somebody
  call my name
And when you realize how they tricked
  you this time
And it's all lies but I'm strung out on
  the wire
In these streets of fire

I live now only with strangers
I talk to only strangers
I walk with angels that have no place
Streets of fire

prove it all night

I've been working real hard trying to get
my hands clean
Tonight we'll drive that dusty road from
Monroe to Angeline
To buy you a gold ring and pretty dress
of blue
Baby, just one kiss will get these things
for you
A kiss to seal our fate tonight
A kiss to prove it all night
Prove it all night
Girl, there's nothing else that we can do
So prove it all night, prove it all night
And girl I'll prove it all night for you

Everybody's got a hunger, a hunger they
can't resist
There's so much that you want, you
deserve much more than this
But if dreams came true oh wouldn't
that be nice
But this ain't no dream we're living
through tonight

Girl, you want it, you take it, you pay
the price
To prove it all night, prove it all night
Prove it all night, babe, and call the
bluff
Prove it all night, prove it all night
Girl, I prove it all night for your love

Baby, tie your hair back in a long white
bow
Meet me in the fields out behind the
dynamo
You hear the voices telling you not to go
They made their choices and they'll
never know
What it means to steal, to cheat, to lie
What it's like to live and die
To prove it all night, prove it all night
Girl, there's nothing else that we can do
So prove it all night, prove it all night
And girl I'll prove it all night for you

Prove It All Night

An baby me + you Ain't we just Alike
yea baby me + you we both save ours for the
little criminals night   okey
do you really think these streets will Allow you
                    your paradise
An honey if dreams came true baby ian't that that
          be nice
you want it you take it you better be ready
          to pay the price

          some 2nd verse

2 lane road black top on 61 / flat strip of blacktop
2 old cowboys open one passin run
cross 500 feet of blacktop headlights two to two
2 swing open the door then baby it goes so quiet
we let the engines roar As we dissolve in it tonight if feels so nice
but something starts screamin   flash our lights
+ something car

dress / you know I'll give my best
     or is this a dream we
this ain't no dream were moving through Mary

baby wants a mustang / stallion

you look so wild tonight   stole beln cheated lied
                         belied   gived
how much you hurt for the ones who stole who cheated
          who lied to prove it
baby maybe you can just give it up without a word

The evolution of "Prove It All Night" beginning with a few lines from the second verse

Prove it

young thing/ little girl on the corner lookin for a friend
young blood   wanna have a friend
        baby just shoot your line + we'll take it
        (to) till the end
        I swing open the door you hop in by my
                side   take
        we let the engine roar we make it till it's
                right   until we blow off the night
        but somethin keeps pushin me inside pushin to...
            (Chorus)

                                                    scared
poss 3rd v.   theres a darkness up ahead + I'm empty
out here   down below (through + through)
It's all just the radios gone dead + girl I don't know
dead   where we can go (I don't know what
(what were gonna do I don't know) were gonna do)
I don't stop baby I can't (don't) (know how) to stop
                I got a hunger I can't resist
        I'm lookin for true, real (real true) love
        I'm lookin for a kiss to (that will) seal my
            (our) fate tonight a kiss to ...

        ▦

poss 2. v.   my baby (little girl) wants a cadillac she
                wants a dress of blue
        honey (baby) if I could I'd get those things for
                can   you
        if dreams came true ar baby wouldn't that
                be nice
        this ain't no dream were movin through
                tonight   magic
        you ain't no dream + baby I ain't your toy
        you want it you take it (got it) you better
        be ready to pay the price to prove...

Tomba Lie

Prove it

baby tie your hair back in a long white bow
meet me in the fields out behind the dynamo
hold me close promise you'll never let me go
we'll burn it all then baby we'll let go
we'll throw it all on one last ride

promise you won't quit promise you'll never let go
baby let 'em fall cause girl they'll never know
what it's like to throw it all on one last ride
+ push to prove it...

A kiss to seal the promises we made tonight

baby tie your hair back in a long white bow
meet me in the night fields out behind the dynamo
you hear their voices calling for you not to go
but girl they made their choices + they'll never know
what it's like to know for just one moment that it's
like you got it right + push to prove it...
to fight for the right to feel like your alive + push ride

the choice is yours you got the right but just believe it...

were drawn till the hit you can use the backseat
for a bed
nobody out here gives a damn whether your alive or dead
oh yes we can ride thes old roam baby what
cose nobody folks in town don't give a damn what goes on
out here they never gonna reach drive into the
heart for the fight

Songs Daddy Render...
Outside Prove it
Something invisible

The third verse emerges.

Prove it (New)

baby I'll buy you a cadillac and a pretty dress
of blue
baby, I'll do my very best to get these things for
(if dreams...) ✱ I got my own kind of hunger
that I can't resist you got so much that
I want
ridin dust roads from Monroe into Angeline
me + Willy ford pullin into Angeline / Caroline
Willy let's b. engines roar now runnin on borrowed time
I got my

I. I work 2 jobs till I get my hands clean
then we'll ride the dust roads from Monroe to Angeline
+ I'll buy you a cadillac (gold) + a pretty dress of blue
sweet thing for just one kiss (I'd swear I'd got)
I'll got... A kiss to seal...

II. Everybodys got theyown hunger somethin they can't resist
I got my own hunger I can't resist
thats so much baby me + you we deserve better more (so much) than this
if dreams...

✱ go my of gold
I'll buy you a cadillac + a pretty blu dress
+ swear I'll get these things for you for just one kiss...

IV. Everybodys got their own hunger somethin they can't resist
theres plenty that I want thes so much that I we've
missed
oh and if dreams come true would that...

III. baby we been trapped on the inside befor were on boy
cause baby out on the outside we can't nobody buy a bed

I/

Ⓐ I've worked 18 jobs till I got my hands clean
we're gonna ride the dust roads from Monroe to Angeline
'cause I got a hunger a hunger I can't resist
theres so much that I want girl right now I want
a kiss to seal...

Ⓑ baby wants a cadilac *ring of gold* she wants a dress of blue
+ honey if I can I get these things for you
if dreams came true Ann wouldn't that be nice
but it ain't no dream we're livin through tonight
you want it you take it you ~~better be a~~ pay the price

Ⓒ so baby tie your hair back in a long white bow
meet me in the fields out behind the dynamo
'cause we been trapped on the inside before
c'mon we even begun
well break out to the outside we can be just
like the ones who sold who cheated who
lied (who chose their sides stood + lived + died
took their chances + lived + died

II/

Ⓐ Baby I've worked 2 jobs just to get my hands clean
tonight I wone drive these dust roads on to Angeline
+ I'll buy you a ~~~~ gold ring + a pretty dress of blue
for just one kiss I'll get these things for you
a kiss

Ⓑ Baby I got a hunger a hunger I can't resist
theres so much that I want too much
that I's *just* need
if dreams came true oh....

the right balance between a garage band and the professionalism required to make good records. Plus, I had a clear idea of what I wanted to hear. I wanted the snare drum to explode and I wanted less separation between the instruments. Also, after the seriousness of *Darkness,* I wanted to give myself a lot more flexibility with the emotional range of the songs I chose. Our shows had always been filled with fun and I didn't want to see that left out this time around.

The first song we cut for *The River* was "Roulette," which I'd written on the tail of the Three Mile Island nuclear accident. It had an appropriately paranoid lyric and an exciting track, but it never made it to the record. Next, we cut "The Ties That Bind," with the band playing in a wood-paneled studio with open mikes over the drumkit to get that live resonance. Everything was splashing around. We weren't in complete control of the way everything sounded, but that was the idea.

Minus—at the moment—any grand strategy, I was just trying to write some good songs. If anything, I wanted to create songs that would sound good played by a bar band. To me, that was basically what we remained. All the years I'd been performing, I'd often start the show with something that sounded like it came out of the garage. In the past, these were the kinds of songs that fell by the wayside when we went into the studio to record. For *The River,* I wanted to make sure this part of what I did wouldn't get lost.

After some recording we prepared a single album and handed it in to the record company. When I listened to it later on, I felt that it just wasn't good enough. The songs lacked the kind of unity and conceptual intensity I liked my music to have. So we went back into the studio and another year went by. Many songs were cut, and many were judged not up to par. Part of the problem might have been the less meticulous, more instinctive way that I approached songwriting this

time around. Once you have a few successful records under your belt, you become more aware of people's expectations. You can become too cautious. On *The River* I was determined to let the band play live and let the music happen. Some nights it worked, and some nights it didn't. It was in struggling to reconcile my previous and present recording approaches that the album found its identity. We decided to make *The River* a double record. I'd try for the best of both worlds: more pop songs in a looser conceptual framework.

The River got its emotional depth from its ballads. "Point Blank," "Independence Day," "The River," "Stolen Car" were all song-stories. "Stolen Car" was the predecessor for a good deal of the music I'd be writing in the future. It was inner-directed, psychological; this was the character whose progress I'd soon be following on *Tunnel of Love*. He was the archetype for the male role in my later songs about men and women.

The album got its energy from "Cadillac Ranch," "Hungry Heart," "Two Hearts," "Ramrod," and the other club rockers. This was the music I wrote to provide fuel for our live show and to create a counterbalance to the ballads that began showing up more and more in my work. These songs provided an emotional release and an external point of view before the ballads returned you to the internal lives of the characters.

The River also was my first attempt to write about the commitments of home and marriage. Country music, once again, continued to be important. One night in my hotel room in New York, I started singing Hank Williams's "My Bucket's Got a Hole In It." I drove back to New Jersey that night and sat up in my room writing "The River." I used a narrative folk voice—just a guy in a bar telling his story to the stranger on the next stool. I based the song on the crash of the construction industry in late '70s New Jersey and the hard times that fell on my sister and her family. I watched my brother-in-law lose his good-paying job and work hard to survive without complaint. When my sister first heard it, she came backstage, gave me a hug, and said, "That's my life." That song crystallized my concerns and was a style of writing I'd develop in greater depth and detail on *Nebraska* and *The Ghost of Tom Joad.*

The album closes with a title stolen from a Roy Acuff song. "Wreck on the Highway" is about confronting one's own death and stepping into the adult world where time is finite. On a rainy highway the character witnesses a fatal accident. He drives home, and lying awake that night next to his lover, he realizes that you have a limited number of opportunities to love someone, to do your work, to be a part of something, to parent your children, to do something good.

the ties that bind

You been hurt and you're all cried out
you say
You walk down the street pushing
people outta your way
You packed your bags and all alone you
wanna ride
You don't want nothin', don't need no
one by your side
You're walkin' tough, baby but you're
walkin' blind
To the ties that bind
The ties that bind
Now you can't break the ties that bind

Cheap romance it's all just a crutch

You don't want nothin' that anybody
can touch
You're so afraid of being somebody's
fool
Not walkin' tough, baby not walkin' cool
You walk cool but darlin' can you walk
the line
And face the ties that bind
The ties that bind
Now you can't break the ties that bind

I would rather feel the hurt inside
Yes I would darlin'
Than know the emptiness your heart
must hide
Yes I would darlin', yes I would darlin'

Yes I would baby

You sit and wonder just who's gonna
stop the rain
Who'll ease the sadness, who's gonna
quiet the pain
It's a long dark highway and a thin
white line
Connecting, baby, your heart to mine
We're runnin' now but darlin' we will
stand in time
To face the ties that bind
The ties that bind
Now you can't break the ties that bind
You can't forsake the ties that bind

sherry darling

Your mama's yappin' in the backseat
Tell her to push over and move them
  big feet
Every Monday morning I gotta drive her
  down to the unemployment agency
Well this morning I ain't fighting, tell
  her I give up
Tell her she wins if she'll just shut up
But it's the last time that she's gonna
  be riding with me

CHORUS:
You can tell her there's a hot sun beat-
  ing on the blacktop
She keeps talkin' she'll be walkin' that
  last block
She can take a subway back to the
  ghetto tonight
Well I got some beer and the highway's
  free
And I got you and baby you got me
Hey, hey, hey, what you say, Sherry
  darling

Well there's girls meltin' out on the
  beach
And they're so fine but so out of reach
'Cause I'm stuck in traffic down on
  Fifty-third Street
Now Sherry, my love for you is real
But I didn't count on this package deal
And baby, this car just ain't big enough
  for her and me

(CHORUS)

Well let there be sunlight, let there be
  rain
Let the brokenhearted love again
Sherry, we can run with our arms open
  wide before the tide
To all the girls down at Sacred Heart
And all you operators back in the park
Say hey, hey, hey, what you say, Sherry
  darling
Say hey, hey, what you say, Sherry
  darling

jackson cage

Driving home she grabs something
   to eat
Turns a corner and drives down the
   street
Into a row of houses she just melts
   away
Like the scenery in another man's play
Into a house where the blinds are
   closed
To keep from seeing things she don't
   wanna know
She pulls the blinds and looks out on
   the street
The cool of the night takes the edge off
   the heat
In the Jackson Cage
Down in the Jackson Cage
You can try with all your might
But you're reminded every night
That you been judged and handed life
Down in the Jackson Cage

Every day ends in wasted motion
Just crossed swords on the killing floor
To settle back is to settle without
   knowing
The hard edge that you're settling for
Because there's always just one more
   day
And it's always gonna be that way

Little girl, you've been down here so
   long
I can tell by the way that you move you
   belong to
The Jackson Cage
Down in Jackson Cage
And it don't matter just what you say
Are you tough enough to play the game
   they play
Or will you just do your time and fade
   away
Down into the Jackson Cage

Baby there's nights when I dream of a
   better world
But I wake up so downhearted, girl
I see you feeling so tired and confused
I wonder what it's worth to me or you
Just waiting to see some sun
Never knowing if that day will ever
   come
Left alone standing out on the street
Till you become the hand that turns the
   key down in
Jackson Cage
Down in Jackson Cage
Well darlin', can you understand
The way that they will turn a man
Into a stranger to waste away
Down in the Jackson Cage

Your mamma's yappin in the backseat
    babe cause you tell her to shudup
Every monday mornin I gotta drag her
    to the agency,   all day long
tell   slydown cut plead her case
tell her this mornin I ain't fightin
" "   she wins baby, I give up
" "   it's her last ride in the machine now
        + see

tell her there's a hot sun beatin on the blacktop
    if she keep talkin she'll be walkin that
        last block
    tell her she can take a taxi back to the
        ghetto cause I ain't comin back

                    beer
    I got some wine + the highways free I got you
        + babe you got me   cherry darling
                                    Darlene
    there's a hot sun beatin on the blacktop
    no matter what goes down baby I can't stop
    the music's playin + I won't stop

    (I been thrown out on my own with a head half-broken
        + my radio's blown
    no matter how she trys to shut up

    So your mamma's yappin in the backseat
        lets open the door + kick her out on the street
        hey hey, what ya say Debby May

bridge

so let there be sunlight let there be rain
let there be broken hearts and let them love again
    let the broken hearted love again

they are girls melting on the beach from working boys like me
they wait just out of reach from working boys like us

let us run before the tide with our hearts
        open wide let 'em all come runnin
    & now take it all in

And let the keeper of the secret hearts and all
        you operators down in Bear Park   the park
know that she kids and kraft's you this time
when you have to you let go roll up the
        windows turn the radio low
    and you've learned the music something's for the romance
+ the radio's just a buzz in the background

Tel her she don't stop pleadin' that case
I'm gonna turn up this radio till I blow
    that gun off her face
    don't look

two hearts

I went out walking the other day
Seen a little girl crying along the way
She'd been hurt so bad said she'd
    never love again
Someday your crying, girl, will end
And you'll find once again

CHORUS:
Two hearts are better than one
Two hearts, girl, get the job done
Two hearts are better than one

Once I spent my time playing tough guy
    scenes
But I was living in a world of childish
    dreams
Someday these childish dreams must
    end
To become a man and grow up to
    dream again

Now I believe in the end

(CHORUS)

Sometimes it might seem like it was
    planned
For you to roam empty hearted through
    this land
Though the world turns you hard and
    cold
There's one thing, mister, that I know
That's if you think your heart is stone
And that you're rough enough to whip
    this world alone
Alone, buddy, there ain't no peace of
    mind
That's why I'll keep searching till I find
My special one

(CHORUS)

independence day

Well Papa go to bed now, it's getting
  late
Nothing we can say is gonna change
  anything now
I'll be leaving in the morning from Saint
  Mary's Gate
We wouldn't change this thing even if
  we could somehow
'Cause the darkness of this house has
  got the best of us
There's a darkness in this town that's
  got us too
But they can't touch me now
And you can't touch me now
They ain't gonna do to me
What I watched them do to you

So say good-bye, it's Independence Day
It's Independence Day
All down the line
Just say good-bye, it's Independence
  Day
It's Independence Day this time

Now I don't know what it always was
  with us
We chose the words, and yeah, we drew
  the lines
There was just no way this house could
  hold the two of us
I guess that we were just too much of
  the same kind

Well say good-bye, it's Independence
  Day
It's Independence Day, all boys must
  run away
So say good-bye, it's Independence Day
All men must make their way come
  Independence Day

Now the rooms are all empty down at
  Frankie's joint
And the highway she's deserted clear
  down to Breaker's Point
There's a lot of people leaving town

now, leaving their friends, their
  homes
At night they walk that dark and dusty
  highway all alone

Well Papa go to bed now, it's getting
  late
Nothing we can say can change
  anything now
Because there's just different people
  coming down here now
And they see things in different ways
And soon everything we've known will
  just be swept away

So say good-bye, it's Independence Day
Papa now I know the things you wanted
  that you could not say
But won't you just say good-bye, it's
  Independence Day
I swear I never meant to take those
  things away

you can look [but you better not touch]

Yesterday I went shopping, buddy, down to the mall
Looking for something pretty I could hang on my wall
I knocked over a lamp, before it hit the floor I caught it
A salesman turned around said "Boy, you break that thing, you bought it"

CHORUS:
You can look but you better not touch, boy
You can look but you better not touch, boy
Mess around and you'll end up in Dutch, boy
You can look but you better not, no you better not, no you better not touch

When I came home from work and I switched on channel five
There was a pretty little girly lookin' straight into my eyes
Well I watched as she wiggled back and forth across the screen
She didn't get me excited, she just made me feel mean

(CHORUS)

Well I called up Dirty Annie on the telephone
I took her out to the drive-in just to get her alone
I found a lovers' rendezvous, the music low, set to park
I heard a tappin' on the window and a voice in the dark

(CHORUS)

i wanna marry you

I see you walking, baby, down the street
Pushing that baby carriage at your feet
I see that lonely ribbon in your hair
Tell me am I the man for whom you put
    it there

You never smile, girl, you never speak
You just walk on by, darlin', week after
    week
Raising two kids alone in this mixed-up
    world
Must be a lonely life for a working girl

CHORUS:
Little girl I wanna marry you
Oh yeah, little girl, I wanna marry you
Yes I do, little girl, I wanna marry you

Now honey I don't want to clip your
    wings
But a time comes when two people
    should think of these things
Having a home and a family

Facing up to their responsibilities
They say in the end true love prevails
But in the end true love can't be some
    fairy tale
To say I'll make your dreams come true
    would be wrong
But maybe, darlin', I could help them
    along

(CHORUS)

My daddy said right before he died
That true, true love was just a lie
He went to his grave a broken heart
An unfulfilled life, girl, makes a man
    hard

Oh darlin'
There's something happy and there's
    something sad
'Bout wanting somebody oh so bad
I wear my love, darlin', without shame
I'd be proud if you would wear my name

the river

I come from down in the valley
Where mister, when you're young
They bring you up to do like your daddy
   done
Me and Mary we met in high school
When she was just seventeen
We'd drive out of this valley
Down to where the fields were green
We'd go down to the river
And into the river we'd dive
Oh down to the river we'd ride

Then I got Mary pregnant
And man, that was all she wrote
And for my nineteenth birthday
I got a union card and a wedding coat
We went down to the courthouse
And the judge put it all to rest
No wedding day smiles, no walk down
   the aisle
No flowers, no wedding dress
That night we went down to the river
And into the river we'd dive
Oh down to the river we did ride

I got a job working construction
For the Johnstown Company

But lately there ain't been much work
On account of the economy
Now all them things that seemed so
   important
Well mister, they vanished right into the
   air
Now I just act like I don't remember
Mary acts like she don't care
But I remember us riding in my
   brother's car
Her body tan and wet down at the
   reservoir
At night on them banks I'd lie awake
And pull her close just to feel each
   breath she'd take
Now those memories come back to
   haunt me
They haunt me like a curse
Is a dream a lie if it don't come true
Or is it something worse
That sends me down to the river
Though I know the river is dry
That sends me down to the river tonight
Down to the river
My baby and I
Oh down to the river we ride

point blank

Do you still say your prayers, little
   darlin'
Do you go to bed at night
Prayin' that tomorrow everything will be
   all right
But tomorrows fall in number
In number one by one
You wake up and you're dying
You don't even know what from
Well they shot you point blank
You been shot in the back
Baby, point blank
You been fooled this time, little girl,
   that's a fact
Right between the eyes, baby, point
   blank
Right between the pretty lies that
   they tell
Little girl you fell

You grew up where young girls they
   grow up fast
You took what you were handed and left
   behind what was asked
But what they asked, baby, wasn't right
You didn't have to live that life
I was gonna be your Romeo, you were
   gonna be my Juliet
These days you don't wait on Romeos,
   you wait on that welfare check
And on all the pretty little things that
   you can't ever have

And on all the promises
That always end up point blank
Shot between the eyes
Point blank
Like little white lies you tell to ease the
   pain
You're walkin' in the sights, girl, of
   point blank
And it's one false move and baby the
   lights go out

Once I dreamed we were together again
Baby, you and me
Back home in those old clubs
The way we used to be
We were standin' at the bar and it was
   hard to hear
The band was playin' loud and you
   were shoutin' something in my ear
You pulled my jacket off and as the
   drummer counted four
You grabbed my hand and pulled me
   out on the floor
You just stood there and held me, then
   you started dancin' slow
And as I pulled you tighter I swore I'd
   never let you go
Well I saw you last night down on the
   avenue
Your face was in the shadows but I
   knew that it was you

You were standin' in the doorway out of
   the rain
You didn't answer when I called out
   your name
You just turned and then you looked
   away
Like just another stranger waitin' to get
   blown away
Point blank
Right between the eyes
Point blank
Right between the pretty lies you fell
Point blank
Shot straight through the heart
Yeah, point blank
You've been twisted up till you've
   become just another part of it
Point blank
You're walkin' in the sights
Point blank
Livin' one false move just one false
   move away
Point blank
They caught you in their sights
Point blank
Did you forget how to love, girl, did you
   forget how to fight
Point blank
They must have shot you in the head
'Cause point blank
Bang bang baby you're dead

cadillac ranch

Well there she sits, buddy, just
    a-gleamin' in the sun
There to greet a working man when his
    day is done
I'm gonna pack my pa and I'm gonna
    pack my aunt
I'm gonna take them down to the
    Cadillac Ranch

Eldorado fins, whitewalls and skirts
Rides just like a little bit of heaven
    here on earth
Well buddy when I die throw my body in
    the back
And drive me to the junkyard in my
    Cadillac

Cadillac, Cadillac
Long and dark, shiney and black
Open up your engines, let 'em roar
Tearing up the highway like a big old
    dinosaur

James Dean in that Mercury '49
Junior Johnson runnin' through the
    woods of Caroline

Even Burt Reynolds in that black
    TransAm
All gonna meet down at the Cadillac
    Ranch

Cadillac, Cadillac
Long and dark, shiney and black
Open up your engines, let 'em roar
Tearing up the highway like a big old
    dinosaur

Hey little girlie in the blue jeans so
    tight
Drivin' alone through the Wisconsin
    night
You're my last love, baby, you're my last
    chance
Don't let 'em take me to the Cadillac
    Ranch

Cadillac, Cadillac
Long and dark, shiney and black
Pulled up to my house today
Came and took my little girl away

i'm a rocker

I got a .007 watch and it's a one and
    only
It's got a *I Spy* beeper that tells me
    when you're lonely
I got a Batmobile so I can reach you in
    a fast shake
When your world's in crisis of an
    impendin' heartbreak

Now don't you call James Bond or
    Secret Agent Man
'Cause they can't do it like I can
I'm a rocker, baby, I'm a rocker—every
    day
I'm a rocker, baby, I'm a rocker

If you're hanging from a cliff or you're
    tied to the tracks, girl
Columbo split and you can't find Kojak
True love is broken and your tears are
    fallin' faster
You're sufferin' from a pain in your
    heart or some other natural disaster

Now I don't care what kind of shape
    you're in
If they put up a roadblock I'll parachute
    in

I'm a rocker, baby, I'm a rocker—I'm in
    love
I'm a rocker, baby, I'm a rocker—every
    day
I'm a rocker, baby, I'm a rocker—with
    you

So you fell for some jerk who was tall,
    dark and handsome
Then he kidnapped your heart and now
    he's holdin' it for ransom
Well like a *Mission Impossible* I'm
    gonna go and get it back
You know I woulda taken better care of
    it, baby, than that

Sometimes I get so hot, girl, well I
    can't talk
But when I'm with you I cool off
I'm a rocker, baby, I'm a rocker—and I
    walk
I'm a rocker, baby, I'm a rocker—and I
    talk
I'm a rocker, baby, I'm a rocker—every
    day
I'm a rocker, baby, I'm a rocker—every
    day

fade away

Well now you say you've found another
  man
Who does things to you that I can't
And that no matter what I do it's all
  over now
Between me and you, girl
But I can't believe what you say
No I can't believe what you say
'Cause baby

CHORUS:
I don't wanna fade away
Oh I don't wanna fade away
Tell me what can I do, what can I say
'Cause darlin' I don't wanna fade away

Well now you say that you've made up
  your mind it's been such a long, long
  time since it's been good with us
And that somewhere back along the
  line you lost your love and I lost your
  trust
Now rooms that once were so bright
Are filled with the coming night, darlin'

(CHORUS)

You say it's not easy for you
And that you've been so lonely
While other girls go out doing what they
  want to do
You say that you miss the nights
When we'd go out dancing
The days when you and I walked as two
Well girl I miss them too
Oh I swear that I do
Oh girl

Now baby I don't wanna be just another
  useless memory holding you tight
Or just some other ghost out on the
  street to whom you stop and politely
  speak when you pass on by
Vanishing into the night
Left to vanish into the night
No baby

(CHORUS)

stolen car

I met a little girl and I settled down
In a little house out on the edge of
    town
We got married and swore we'd never
    part
Then little by little we drifted from each
    other's heart

At first I thought it was just restless-
    ness
That would fade as time went by and
    our love grew deep
In the end it was something more I
    guess
That tore us apart and made us weep

And I'm driving a stolen car
Down on Eldridge Avenue
Each night I wait to get caught
But I never do

She asked if I remembered the letters I
    wrote
When our love was young and bold
She said last night she read those
    letters
And they made her feel one hundred
    years old

And I'm driving a stolen car
On a pitch-black night
And I'm telling myself I'm gonna be all
    right
But I ride by night and I travel in fear
That in this darkness I will disappear

r a m r o d

Hey little dolly with the blue jeans on
I wanna ramrod with you, honey, till
    half-past dawn
Let your hair down, mama, and pick up
    this beat
Come on and meet me tonight down on
    Bluebird Street
I've been working all week, I'm up to my
    neck in hock
Come Saturday night I let my ramrod
    rock

She's a hot-stepping hemi with a four
    on the floor
She's a roadrunner engine in a '32 Ford
Late at night when I'm dead on the line
I swear I think of your pretty face when
    I let her unwind
Well look over yonder, see them city
    lights

Come on little dolly 'n' go ramroddin'
    tonight

Come on, come on, come on little baby
Come on, come on, let's shake it tonight
Come on, come on, come on little sugar
Dance with your daddy and we'll go
    ramroddin' tonight

Hey little dolly won't you say you will
Meet me tonight up on top of the hill
Well just a few miles 'cross the county
    line
There's a cute little chapel nestled
    down in the pines
Say you'll be mine, little girl, I'll put my
    foot to the floor
Give me the word now, sugar, we'll go
    ramroddin' forevermore

the price you pay

You make up your mind, you choose the
  chance you take
You ride to where the highway ends and
  the desert breaks
Out on to an open road you ride until
  the day
You learn to sleep at night with the
  price you pay

Now with their hands held high they
  reached out for the open skies
And in one last breath they built the
  roads they'd ride to their death
Driving on through the night, unable to
  break away
From the restless pull of the price you
  pay

CHORUS:

Oh the price you pay, oh the price you
  pay
Now you can't walk away from the price
  you pay

Now they'd come so far and they'd
  waited so long
Just to end up caught in a dream where
  everything goes wrong
Where the dark of night holds back the
  light of the day
And you've gotta stand and fight for the
  price you pay

(CHORUS)

Little girl down on the strand
With that pretty little baby in your
  hands

Do you remember the story of the
  promised land
How he crossed the desert sands
And could not enter the chosen land
On the banks of the river he stayed
To face the price you pay

So let the game start, you better run,
  you little wild heart
You can run through all the nights and
  all the days
But just across the county line
A stranger passing through put up a
  sign
That counts the men fallen away
To the price you pay
And girl before the end of the day
I'm gonna tear it down and throw it
  away

drive all night

When I lost you, honey, sometimes I
    think I lost my guts too
And I wish God would send me a word,
    send me something I'm afraid to
    lose
Lying in the heat of the night like
    prisoners all our lives
I get shivers down my spine
And all I wanna do is hold you tight

CHORUS:
I swear I'd drive all night again
Just to buy you some shoes
And to taste your tender charms
And I just wanna sleep tonight again in
    your arms

Tonight there's fallen angels and
    they're waiting for us down in the
    street
Tonight there's calling strangers, hear
    them crying in defeat

Let them go, let them go, let them go
    do their dances of the dead (let 'em
    go right ahead)
You just dry your eyes and c'mon,
    c'mon, c'mon, let's go to bed, baby,
    baby, baby

(CHORUS)

There's machines and there's fire, baby,
    waiting on the edge of town
They're out there for hire but baby, they
    can't hurt us now
'Cause you've got, you've got, you've
    got my love, you've got my love, girl
Through the wind, through the rain, the
    snow, the wind, the rain
You've got, you've got my love
Heart and soul

nebrask

wreck on the highway

Last night I was out driving
Coming home at the end of the working
    day
I was riding alone through the drizzling
    rain
On a deserted stretch of a county two-
    lane
When I came upon a wreck on the
    highway

There was blood and glass all over
And there was nobody there but me
As the rain tumbled down hard and
    cold
I seen a young man lying by the side of
    the road
He cried "Mister, won't you help me
    please?"

An ambulance finally came and took
    him to Riverside
I watched as they drove him away
And I thought of a girlfriend or a young
    wife
And a state trooper knocking in the
    middle of the night
To say your baby died in a wreck on the
    highway

Sometimes I sit up in the darkness
And I watch my baby as she sleeps
Then I climb in bed and I hold her tight
I just lay there awake in the middle of
    the night
Thinking 'bout the wreck on the
    highway

highway patrolman

My name is Joe Roberts, I work for the
state
I'm a sergeant out of Perrineville,
barracks number eight
I always done an honest job, as honest
as I could
I got a brother named Frankie and
Frankie ain't no good

Now ever since we was young kids it's
been the same comedown
I get a call over the shortwave Frankie's
in trouble downtown
Well if it was any other man I'd just put
him straight away
But when it's your brother sometimes
you look the other way

Me and Frankie laughin' and drinkin'
Nothin' feels better than blood on blood
Takin' turns dancin' with Maria
As the band played "Night of the
Johnstown Flood"
I catch him when he's strayin' like any
brother would
Man turns his back on his family, well
he just ain't no good

Well Frankie went in the army back in
1965
I got a farm deferment, settled down,
took Maria for my wife
But them wheat prices kept on droppin'
Till it was like we were gettin' robbed
Frankie came home in '68 and me I
took this job

Yeah, we're laughin' and drinkin'
Nothin' feels better than blood on blood
Takin' turns dancin' with Maria
As the band played "Night of the
Johnstown Flood"
I catch him when he's strayin', teach
him how to walk that line
Man turns his back on his family, he
ain't no friend of mine

The night was like any other, I got a call
'bout quarter to nine
There was trouble in a roadhouse out on
the Michigan line
There was a kid lyin' on the floor lookin'
bad, bleedin' hard from his head
There was a girl cryin' at a table, it was
Frank, they said

Well I went out and I jumped in my car
and I hit the lights
I must of drove 110 through Michigan
county that night
It was out at the crossroads down
'round Willow bank
Seen a Buick with Ohio plates, behind
the wheel was Frank
Well I chased him through them county
roads till a sign said "Canadian
border 5 miles from here"
I pulled over the side of the highway
and watched his taillights disappear

Me and Frankie laughin' and drinkin'
Nothin' feels better than blood on blood
Takin' turns dancin' with Maria
As the band played "Night of the
Johnstown Flood"
I catch him when he's strayin' like any
brother would
Man turns his back on his family, well
he just ain't no good

state trooper

New Jersey Turnpike, ridin' on a wet
    night
'Neath the refinery's glow out where the
    great black rivers flow
License, registration, I ain't got none
But I got a clear conscience 'bout the
    things that I done
Mister state trooper, please don't stop
    me

Maybe you got a kid, maybe you got a
    pretty wife
The only thing that I got's been
    botherin' me my whole life
Mister state trooper, please don't stop
    me

In the wee wee hours your mind gets
    hazy
Radio relay towers lead me to my baby
Radio's jammed up with talk show
    stations
It's just talk talk talk talk till you lose
    your patience
Mister state trooper, please don't stop
    me

Hey somebody out there, listen to my
    last prayer
Hi ho silver-o deliver me from nowhere

my father's house

Last night I dreamed that I was a child
Out where the pines grow wild and tall
I was trying to make it home through
    the forest
Before the darkness falls

I heard the wind rustling through the
    trees
And ghostly voices rose from the fields
I ran with my heart pounding down that
    broken path
With the devil snappin' at my heels

I broke through the trees and there in
    the night
My father's house stood shining hard
    and bright
The branches and brambles tore my
    clothes and scratched my arms
But I ran till I fell shaking in his arms

I awoke and I imagined the hard things
    that pulled us apart

Will never again, sir, tear us from each
    other's hearts
I got dressed and to that house I did
    ride
From out on the road I could see its
    window shining in light

I walked up the steps and stood on the
    porch
A woman I didn't recognize came and
    spoke to me through a chained door
I told her my story and who I'd come for
She said "I'm sorry, son, but no one by
    that name lives here anymore"

My father's house shines hard and
    bright
It stands like a beacon calling me in
    the night
Calling and calling so cold and alone
Shining 'cross this dark highway where
    our sins lie unatoned

reason to believe

Seen a man standin' over a dead dog
  lyin' by the highway in a ditch
He's lookin' down kinda puzzled pokin'
  that dog with a stick
Got his car door flung open, he's
  standin' out on Highway 31
Like if he stood there long enough that
  dog'd get up and run
Struck me kinda funny, seem kinda
  funny, sir, to me
Still at the end of every hard day people
  find some reason to believe

Now Mary Lou loved Johnny with a love
  mean and true
She said "Baby I'll work for you every
  day and bring my money home
  to you"

One day he up and left her and ever
  since that
She waits down at the end of that dirt
  road for young Johnny to come back
Struck me kinda funny, funny, yeah,
  indeed
How at the end of every hard-earned
  day people find some reason to
  believe

Take a baby to the river, Kyle William
  they called him
Wash the baby in the water, take away
  little Kyle's sin
In a whitewash shotgun shack an old
  man passes away
Take the body to the graveyard and over
  him they pray

Lord won't you tell us, tell us what does
  it mean
At the end of every hard-earned day you
  can find some reason to believe

Congregation gathers down by the river
  side
Preacher stands with a Bible, groom
  stands waitin' for his bride
Congregation gone and the sun sets
  behind a weepin' willow tree
Groom stands alone and watches the
  river rush on so effortlessly
Wonderin' where can his baby be
Still at the end of every hard-earned day
  people find some reason to believe

born in the u.s.a.

no surrender

We busted out of class, had to get away
from those fools
We learned more from a three-minute
record, baby, than we ever learned in
school
Tonight I hear the neighborhood drummer sound
I can feel my heart begin to pound
You say you're tired and you just want
to close your eyes
And follow your dreams down

We made a promise we swore we'd
always remember
No retreat, baby, no surrender
Like soldiers in the winter's night with a
vow to defend
No retreat, baby, no surrender

Now young faces grow sad and old
And hearts of fire grow cold
We swore blood brothers against the
wind
Now I'm ready to grow young again
And hear your sister's voice calling us
home

Across the open yards
Well maybe we could cut some place of
our own
With these drums and these guitars

CHORUS:
'Cause we made a promise we swore
we'd always remember
No retreat, baby, no surrender
Blood brothers in the stormy night with
a vow to defend
No retreat, baby, no surrender

Now on the street tonight the lights
grow dim
The walls of my room are closing in
There's a war outside still raging
You say it ain't ours anymore to win
I want to sleep beneath peaceful skies
in my lover's bed
With a wide open country in my eyes
and these romantic dreams in my
head

(CHORUS)

bobby jean

Well I came by your house the other day
Your mother said you went away
She said there was nothing that I could
　　have done
There was nothing nobody could say
Me and you we've known each other
Ever since we were sixteen
I wished I would have known
I wished I could have called you
Just to say good-bye, Bobby Jean

Now you hung with me when all the
　　others
Turned away, turned up their noses
We liked the same music, we liked the
　　same bands
We liked the same clothes
We told each other that we were the
　　wildest
The wildest things we'd ever seen
Now I wished you would have told me
I wished I could have talked to you

Just to say good-bye, Bobby Jean

Now we went walking in the rain
Talking about the pain that from the
　　world we hid
Now there ain't nobody nowhere nohow
Gonna ever understand me the way you
　　did

Maybe you'll be out there on that road
　　somewhere
In some bus or train traveling along
In some motel room there'll be a radio
　　playing
And you'll hear me sing this song
Well if you do you'll know I'm thinking
　　of you
And all the miles in between
And I'm just calling one last time
Not to change your mind, but just to
　　say I miss you, baby
Good luck, good-bye, Bobby Jean

Overleaf: Born in the U.S.A. photo shoot, basement, Rumson, New Jersey

Glory Days

I had A friend was a big baseball player
        back in high school
he could throw that speedball by you make
        make you look like A fool boy
saw him the other night at this roadside bar
        I was walkin' in he was walkin' out
we went back inside sat down had a few
        drinks but all he kept talkin
about was

        glory days   well they pass you by
glory days   in the wink of A young girls
        eye   glory days   glory days

theres a girl lives up the block   back in school
        she used to turn all the boys heads
Sometimes on a friday or saturday I stop
        by + have a few drinks after she's put
her kids to bed
her and her husband Bobby   well they split up
I guess it's 2 yrs gone by now
talkin bout old times + just when she feels like cryin'
        she starts laughin (thinkin) about

        glory days they'll pass you by
glory days in the wink of a young mans eyes
        glory days glory days

my old man sits down at the legion hall at the bar and A
they sit around talkin 'bout how everybody going to hell + the way it
        was back in war II
now people get sloppy on the flag + put us and I get drunk all the time
        man that was a time

Fred of my dads   on the line

My old man worked 20 yrs for the company + they
        let him go
Now everywhere he goes or lookin for a job they s r tell
        him he's to old
I was 9 yrs old when he was layin in them firewalls
        on at the Metuchen Ford plant Assembly line
Now he just sits on a stool at the bar down at the
        legion hall but I can tell from the look on
        his face exactly whats on his mind
                                            over time

        glory days, ~~he ~~ gone bad
        glory days he never had
        glory days   glory days

~~Sometimes on a summer night I'll sit~~
~~out on the porch watchin the new ball~~
~~   with ~~

~~And the air will be warm + still~~
And I hope when I get old I dont sit around
        thinkin bout all this stuff but I probably
        probably will
just sittin back tryin to recapture just a little
        bit of the glory of
time slips away and leaves you with nothin
        but borin stories of
glory days   yea they'll pass you by
glory days   in the wink of a young girls eye
        glory days glory days

[Sometimes
I think I'm gonna down to the well + I'm gonna drink
till I get my fill

dancing in the dark

I get up in the evening
And I ain't got nothing to say
I come home in the morning
I go to bed feeling the same way
I ain't nothing but tired
Man, I'm just tired and bored with
    myself
Hey there baby, I could use just a little
    help

CHORUS:
You can't start a fire
You can't start a fire without a spark
This gun's for hire
Even if we're just dancing in the dark

Message keeps getting clearer
Radio's on and I'm moving 'round the
    place

I check my look in the mirror
I wanna change my clothes, my hair,
    my face
Man, I ain't getting nowhere
Just living in a dump like this
There's something happening some-
    where
Baby I just know that there is

(CHORUS)

You sit around getting older
There's a joke here somewhere and it's
    on me
I'll shake this world off my shoulders
Come on, baby, the laugh's on me

Stay on the streets of this town
And they'll be carving you up all right
They say you gotta stay hungry

Hey, baby, I'm just about starving
    tonight
I'm dying for some action
I'm sick of sitting 'round here trying to
    write this book
I need a love reaction
Come on now, baby, gimme just
    one look

You can't start a fire
Sitting 'round crying over a broken
    heart
This gun's for hire
Even if we're just dancing in the dark
You can't start a fire
Worrying about your little world falling
    apart
This gun's for hire
Even if we're just dancing in the dark

my hometown

I was eight years old and running with
A dime in my hand
Into the bus stop to pick up a paper
For my old man
I'd sit on his lap in that big old Buick
And steer as we drove through town
He'd tousle my hair and say "Son take
     a good look around
This is your hometown"
This is your hometown
This is your hometown
This is your hometown

In '65 tension was running high
At my high school
There was a lot of fights between the
     black and white

There was nothing you could do
Two cars at a light on a Saturday night
In the backseat there was a gun
Words were passed, in a shotgun blast
Troubled times had come
To my hometown
My hometown
My hometown
My hometown

Now Main Street's whitewashed
     windows
And vacant stores
Seems like there ain't nobody
Wants to come down here no more
They're closing down the textile mill
Across the railroad tracks

Foreman says these jobs are going boys
And they ain't coming back
To your hometown
Your hometown
Your hometown
Your hometown

Last night me and Kate we laid in bed
Talking about getting out
Packing up our bags maybe
Heading south
I'm thirty-five, we got a boy
Of our own now
Last night I sat him up behind the
     wheel
And said "Son take a good look around
This is your hometown"

tunnel

of

love

step back with more reflective work. In 1987, with this in mind, I decided to reintroduce myself to my fans as a songwriter.

I set up my recording equipment above my garage in Rumson, New Jersey, and began demoing. I wanted to go back to the intimacy of home recording. I started to write about something I'd never written about in depth before: men and women.

The songs for *Tunnel of Love* came out of a single place in a short period of time. The songs and the record happened very fast. Most of the recording was done over the course of three weeks. The writing was not painful, and though some thought so, not literally autobiographical. Instead, it uncovered an inner life and unresolved feelings that I had carried inside me for a long time. I was thirty-seven years old; I didn't see myself with suitcase in hand, guitar at my side, on the tour bus for the rest of my life. I assumed my audience was moving on, as I was.

The beginnings of *Tunnel of Love* go back to "Stolen Car" from *The River.* The song's character, drifting through the night, first confronts the angels and devils that drive him towards his love and keep him from ever reaching her. That character became the main voice of my new record; he embodied the transition my characters made into confronting the more intimate struggles of adult love.

Musically, *Tunnel of Love* was shaped by my recording process. I cut the songs live to a rhythm track, which provided the stability and the sense of a ticking clock. The passage of time was a subtext of my new stories. My characters were no longer kids. There was the possibility of life passing them by, of the things they needed—love, a home—rushing out the open window of all those cars I'd placed them in.

The center of *Tunnel of Love* is "Brilliant Disguise." Trust is a fragile thing; it requires allowing others to see as much of ourselves as we have the courage to reveal. But you drop one mask and find another behind it, until you begin to doubt your own feelings about who you are. It's the twin issues of love and identity that form the core of *Tunnel of Love*.

"Brilliant Disguise," "Two Faces," "One Step Up," "Cautious Man," all tell the story of men whose inner sense of themselves is in doubt. "Tougher Than the Rest," "All That Heaven Will Allow," "Walk Like a Man," "Valentine's Day" have characters struggling toward some tenuous commitment. Knowing that when you make that stand, the clock starts, and you walk not just at your partner's side, but alongside your own mortal self. You name the things beyond your work that will give your life its context and meaning. You promise to be faithful to them. The struggle to uncover who you are and to reach that moment and hold on to it, along with the destructive desire to leave it in ruins, binds together the songs on *Tunnel of Love*.

For twenty years I'd written about the man on the road. On *Tunnel of Love* that changed, and my music turned to the hopes and fears of the man in the house.

tougher than the rest

Well it's Saturday night
You're all dressed up in blue
I been watching you awhile
Maybe you been watching me too
So somebody ran out
Left somebody's heart in a mess
Well if you're looking for love
Honey I'm tougher than the rest

Some girls they want a handsome Dan
Or some good-lookin' Joe, on their arm
Some girls like a sweet-talkin' Romeo
Well 'round here baby
I learned you get what you can get
So if you're rough enough for love
Honey I'm tougher than the rest

The road is dark
And it's a thin thin line

But I want you to know I'll walk it for
   you any time
Maybe your other boyfriends
Couldn't pass the test
Well if you're rough and ready for love
Honey I'm tougher than the rest

Well it ain't no secret
I've been around a time or two
Well I don't know, baby, maybe you've
   been around too
Well there's another dance
All you gotta do is say yes
And if you're rough and ready for love
Honey I'm tougher than the rest
If you're rough enough for love
Baby I'm tougher that the rest

all that heaven will allow

I got a dollar in my pocket
There ain't a cloud up above
I got a picture in a locket
That says baby I love you
Well if you didn't look then, boys
Then fellas don't go lookin' now
Well here she comes a-walkin'
All that heaven will allow

Say hey there Mister Bouncer
Now all I wanna do is dance
But I swear I left my wallet
Back home in my workin' pants
C'mon, Slim, slip me in, man
I'll make it up to you somehow
I can't be late, I got a date
With all that heaven will allow

Rain and storm and dark skies
Well now they don't mean a thing
If you got a girl that loves you
And who wants to wear your ring
So c'mon Mister Trouble
We'll make it through you somehow
We'll fill this house with all the love
All that heaven will allow

Now some may wanna die young, man
Young and gloriously
Get it straight now, mister
Hey buddy that ain't me
'Cause I got something on my mind
That sets me straight and walkin'
    proud
And I want all the time
All that heaven will allow

Tougher Than the Rest

Some girls want a handsome Dan
    or a pretty boy Joe
Always on their arms they need a
    real Valentino
if you lookin for good looks (beauty) ~~let~~ well I
    ain't gonna win no beauty test
but if you rough enuf for love call on me
    The Bigger the Rest

Some girls say they gots them hum hum styles
        a real he-man
they want a tiny tiny Buddy
        or a real Tarzan
if you want Mr Rambo then baby be
    my guest
but if you rough + ready for love call on me

Some girls want flowers + romance every day
            they go
They want a sweet soft talkin sensible
        Romio
well it's pretty you want then baby

I gotta confess   ✱ (days of youth)
        proof   truth
        test   proof
    unless
All you got to say is yes

if you rough + ready for a real love

you know baby I been around a time or two

"Tougher Than the Rest"—originally written as a rockabilly song

You all dressed up + baby it's Saturday night
I been watchin you awhile + I got something
To say if you thinks it's alright

Gimme a chance baby I'll prove to ya

You gave your heart before + and
nobody passed the test
but I'm rough + ready...

some girls want happy kings A + joe
A Romeo
I ain't no Romeo + baby you aint no Juliet
but if my my for love baby

I know you been heart + time or two
I don't care baby, I
been around too

there's one more dance
we got another dance baby, + all you gotta
say is yes c'mon for...

I know you seen me around too

Now your Romeos are all gone + so are my Juliets

I know you've had men to tell you all
the things you want to hear
whisper soft sweet pretty words in your ear
then when the daylight comes they run
+ leave your heart in a mess

I know you been disapointed once or twice

spare parts

Bobby said he'd pull out, Bobby stayed in
Janey had a baby, it wasn't any sin
They were set to marry on a summer day
Bobby got scared and he ran away
Jane moved in with her ma out on Shawnee Lake
She sighed "Ma sometimes my whole life feels like one big mistake"
She settled in in a back room, time passed on
Later that winter a son come along

CHORUS:
Spare parts
And broken hearts
Keep the world turnin' around

Now Janey walked that baby across the floor night after night
But she was a young girl and she missed the party lights
Meanwhile in South Texas in a dirty oil patch
Bobby heard 'bout his son bein' born and swore he wasn't ever goin' back

(CHORUS)

Janey heard about a woman over in Calverton
Put her baby in the river, let the river roll on
She looked at her boy in the crib where he lay
Got down on her knees, cried till she prayed

Mist was on the water, low run the tide
Janey held her son down at the river side
Waist deep in the water, how bright the sun shone
She lifted him in her arms and carried him home
As he lay sleeping in her bed Janey took a look around at everything
Went to a drawer in her bureau and got out her old engagement ring
Took out her wedding dress, tied that ring up in its sash
Went straight down to the pawnshop, man, and walked out with some good cold cash

(CHORUS)

cautious man

Bill Horton was a cautious man of the
road
He walked lookin' over his shoulder and
remained faithful to its code
When something caught his eye he'd
measure his need
And then very carefully he'd proceed

Billy met a young girl in the early days
of May
It was there in her arms he let his
cautiousness slip away
In their lovers' twilight as the evening
sky grew dim
He'd lay back in her arms and laugh at
what had happened to him

On his right hand Billy'd tattooed the
word love and on his left hand was
the word fear
And in which hand he held his fate was
never clear
Come Indian summer he took his young
lover for his bride
And with his own hands built her a
great house down by the river side

Now Billy was an honest man, he
wanted to do what was right

He worked hard to fill their lives with
happy days and loving nights
Alone on his knees in the darkness for
steadiness he'd pray
For he knew in a restless heart the
seed of betrayal lay

One night Billy awoke from a terrible
dream callin' his wife's name
She lay breathing beside him in a
peaceful sleep, a thousand miles
away
He got dressed in the moonlight and
down to the highway he strode
When he got there he didn't find
nothing but road

Billy felt a coldness rise up inside him
that he couldn't name
Just as the words tattooed 'cross his
knuckles he knew would always
remain
At their bedside he brushed the hair
from his wife's face as the moon
shone on her skin so white
Filling their room in the beauty of God's
fallen light

brilliant disguise

I hold you in my arms
As the band plays
What are those words whispered, baby
Just as you turn away
I saw you last night
Out on the edge of town
I wanna read your mind
To know just what I've got in
This new thing I've found
So tell me what I see
When I look in your eyes
Is that you, baby
Or just a brilliant disguise

I heard somebody call your name
From underneath our willow
I saw something tucked in shame
Underneath your pillow

Well I've tried so hard, baby
But I just can't see
What a woman like you
Is doing with me
So tell me who I see
When I look in your eyes
Is that you, baby
Or just a brilliant disguise

Now look at me, baby
Struggling to do everything right
And then it falls apart
When out go the lights
I'm just a lonely pilgrim
I walk this world in wealth
I wanna know if it's you I don't trust
'Cause I damn sure don't trust myself

Now you play the loving woman
I'll play the faithful man
But just don't look too close
Into the palm of my hand
We stood at the altar
The gypsy swore our future was right
But come the wee wee hours
Well maybe, baby, the gypsy lied
So when you look at me
You better look hard and look twice
Is that me baby
Or just a brilliant disguise

Tonight our bed is cold
I'm lost in the darkness of our love
God have mercy on the man
Who doubts what he's sure of

one step up

Woke up this morning, the house was
  cold
Checked the furnace, she wasn't
  burnin'
Went out and hopped in my old Ford
Hit the engine but she ain't turnin'
We've given each other some hard
  lessons lately
But we ain't learnin'
We're the same sad story, that's a fact
One step up and two steps back

Bird on a wire outside my motel room
But he ain't singin'
Girl in white outside a church in June
But the church bells they ain't ringin'
I'm sittin' here in this bar tonight
But all I'm thinkin' is
I'm the same old story, same old act
One step up and two steps back

It's the same thing night on night

Who's wrong, baby, who's right
Another fight and I slam the door on
Another battle in our dirty little war
When I look at myself I don't see
The man I wanted to be
Somewhere along the line I slipped off
  track
I'm caught movin' one step up and two
  steps back

There's a girl across the bar
I get the message she's sendin'
Mmm, she ain't lookin' too married
And me, well honey, I'm pretending
Last night I dreamed I held you in my
  arms
The music was never ending
We danced as the evening sky faded to
  black
One step up and two steps back

when you're alone

Times were tough, love was not enough
So you said "Sorry Johnny I'm gone gone
     gone"
You said my act was funny
But we both knew what was missing,
     honey
So you lit out on your own
Now that pretty form that you've got,
     baby
Will make sure you get along
But you're gonna find out some day,
     honey

CHORUS:
When you're alone you're alone
When you're alone you're alone
When you're alone you're alone

When you're alone you ain't nothing but
     alone

Now I was young and pretty on the
     mean streets of the city
And I fought to make 'em my home
With just the shirt on my back I left and
     swore I'd never look back
And man I was gone gone gone
But there's things that'll knock you
     down you don't even see coming
And send you crawling like a baby back
     home
You're gonna find out that day, sugar—

(CHORUS)

I knew some day your runnin' would be
     through
And you'd think back on me and you
And your love would be strong
You'd forget all about the bad and think
     only of all the laughs that we had
And you'd wanna come home
Now it ain't hard feelings or nothin',
     sugar
That ain't what's got me singing this
     song
It's just nobody knows, honey, where
     love goes
But when it goes it's gone gone

(CHORUS)

valentine's day

I'm driving a big lazy car rushin' up the
    highway in the dark
I got one hand steady on the wheel and
    one hand's tremblin' over my heart
It's pounding, baby, like it's gonna bust
    right on through
And it ain't gonna stop till I'm alone
    again with you

A friend of mine became a father last
    night
When we spoke in his voice I could hear
    the light
Of the skies and the rivers the timber-
    wolf in the pines
And that great jukebox out on Route 39
They say he travels fastest who travels
    alone
But tonight I miss my girl, mister,
    tonight I miss my home

Is it the sound of the leaves
Left blown by the wayside
That's got me out here on this spooky
    old highway tonight

Is it the cry of the river
With the moonlight shining through
That ain't what scares me, baby
What scares me is losin' you

They say if you die in your dreams you
    really die in your bed
But, honey, last night I dreamed my
    eyes rolled straight back in my head
And God's light came shinin' on
    through
I woke up in the darkness scared and
    breathin' and born anew
It wasn't the cold river bottom I felt
    rushing over me
It wasn't the bitterness of a dream that
    didn't come true
It wasn't the wind in the gray fields I
    felt rushing through my arms
No no baby it was you
So hold me close, honey, say you're
    forever mine
And tell me you'll be my lonely
    valentine

human
touch

Go west, young man. On Hollywood Boulevard.

fter *Tunnel of Love* was released in 1987 and I toured in 1988, I spent the

next two years doing very little musically. These were the years in which

I saw my family come together. We lived in New York for a while, then we

moved to California. I always loved the West, since I first drove through

with my manager, Tinker, in the early '70s. When I had free time, I'd head

for Arizona and drift through the state on a motorcycle. I'd spent some time in California, since my

parents had moved there twenty-five years before. I had a younger sister in Los Angeles, and in the

early '80s I bought a small bungalow in the Hollywood Hills.

By 1989 Patti and I were looking for a change of scenery and a fresh start. After a stint in New

York City, I realized I still craved some open space. In Los Angeles I could still have my cars and

215

motorcycles, be thirty minutes from the mountains, ocean, and desert, meet some new people, and relax amidst the anonymity of a big city.

Human Touch began as an exercise to get myself back into writing and recording. I wrote a variety of music in genres that I had always liked: soul, rock, pop, R&B. The record, once again, took awhile because I was finding my way to the songs. I also worked for the first time with musicians other than the E Street Band. I felt I needed to see what other people brought with them into the studio and how my music would be affected by collaborating with different talents and personalities.

Roy "The Professor" Bittan—born to be wild

One day in LA Roy Bittan played me a couple of pieces of music that he'd written. I liked them and told him I'd be interested in writing lyrics to them. One of them became "Roll of the Dice," the other became "Real World." I had never collaborated with another songwriter on any of my other records. I was looking for something to get me going; Roy was enthusiastic and had good ideas. He soon joined the production team of *Human Touch,* with Jon and Chuck.

The record took shape when Roy and I would play together in my garage apartment and make tapes of song and arrangement ideas I came up with. Then we'd go into the studio and set up what essentially was a two-man band. I would sing and play guitar; Roy would play the keyboards and

With Patti in New Jersey

bass. Together we'd perform to a drum track. The two of us could create an entire band sound live in the studio. That way we got a good sense of what songs might work, and those were the ideas we developed. Then musicians would come in and play to what we recorded, or we'd play with them and record the songs live. Very often we'd do both and pick what worked the best.

Human Touch was another record that evolved slowly. It took awhile for the songs on the album to shape themselves into a cohesive whole. In "Human Touch," "Soul Driver," and "Real World," people search to find some emotional contact, some modest communion, some physical and sexual connection. But to receive what love delivers, they have to surrender themselves to each other and accept fate. This tension is at the heart of *Human Touch*.

Writers and artists create little worlds and control them. You do that well enough, and you begin to believe you can live in one of them. But the real world doesn't work that way. Love levels the playing field, you can't predict its outcome, and the same rules apply to all. Both *Human Touch* and *Lucky Town* came out of a moment in which to find what I needed, I was going to have to let things go, change, try new things, make mistakes—just live.

At the end of the *Human Touch* album I still felt I needed another song. So I wrote "Living Proof," about the common strength it takes to constitute a family. Children are the "living proof" of our belief in one another, that love is real. They are faith and hope transformed into flesh and blood.

Once I had written "Living Proof," over the next three weeks I wrote and recorded an entirely new record. It was a release from the long process of making *Human Touch*. I set up the home recording equipment and everything came together very quickly, as on *Nebraska* and *Tunnel of Love. Lucky Town* had the ease that came with the relaxed writing and recording of its songs.

"Better Days," "Book of Dreams," and "Leap of Faith" were all songs about second chances. The characters return from broken love affairs and self-doubt and find the tempered optimism to take another shot. "Local Hero" takes an ironic look at "the slings and arrows of outrageous fortune," while "Leap of Faith" is a sexually humorous glimpse at love and resilience. "If I Should Fall

Behind" was one of my best songs about the dedication to one another that comes with love. "The Big Muddy" explores human frailty and the morally ambiguous territory that comes with adulthood.

Scenes from the Persian Gulf War and gang warfare in Los Angeles open "Souls of the Departed." In the song, the character's desire to protect the things he loves most from the violent world around him is undeniable. But the underbelly of that impulse, along with economic injustice, is one of the things that has led us to the racially segregated society we live in. The father in "Souls of the Departed" wrestles with his own hypocrises about the choices he has made for his family in contrast to his beliefs.

Lucky Town closes with "My Beautiful Reward." A man searches for something unnameable, then, slipping between life and death, transforms into a bird flying over gray fields with "the cold wind at my back."

Human Touch and *Lucky Town* were both about the blessings and the unanswerable questions that come with adult life, mortality, and human love.

human touch

You and me we were the pretenders
We let it all slip away
In the end what you don't surrender
Well the world just strips away

Girl, ain't no kindness in the face of
    strangers
Ain't gonna find no miracles here
Well you can wait on your blessings, my
    darlin'
But I got a deal for you right here

I ain't lookin' for prayers or pity
I ain't comin' 'round searchin' for a
    crutch
I just want someone to talk to
And a little of that human touch
Just a little of that human touch

Ain't no mercy on the streets of this
    town
Ain't no bread from heavenly skies
Ain't nobody drawin' wine from this
    blood
It's just you and me tonight

Tell me in a world without pity

Do you think what I'm askin's too much
I just want something to hold on to
And a little of that human touch
Just a little of that human touch

Oh girl, that feeling of safety you prize
Well it comes with a hard hard price
You can't shut off the risk and the pain
Without losin' the love that remains
We're all riders on this train

So you been broken and you been hurt
Show me somebody who ain't
Yeah I know I ain't nobody's bargain
But hell a little touch-up
And a little paint . . .

You might need somethin' to hold on to
When all the answers they don't
    amount to much
Somebody that you can just talk to
And a little of that human touch

Baby in a world without pity
Do you think what I'm askin's too much
I just want to feel you in my arms
And share a little of that human touch

soul driver

Rode through forty nights of the
     gospel's rain
Black sky pourin' snakes, frogs
And love in vain
You were down where the river grows
     wider
Baby let me be your soul driver

Well if something in the air feels a little
     unkind
Don't worry darlin'
It'll slip your mind
I'll be your gypsy joker, your shotgun
     rider
Baby let me be your soul driver

Now no one knows which way love's
     wheel turns
Will we hit it rich
Or crash and burn
Does fortune wait or just the black
     hand of fate
This love potion's all we've got
One toast before it's too late

If the angels are unkind or the season
     is dark
Or if in the end
Love just falls apart
Then here's to our destruction
Baby let me be your soul driver

57 channels [and nothin' on]

I bought a bourgeois house in the
  Hollywood hills
With a trunkload of hundred thousand
  dollar bills
Man came by to hook up my cable TV
We settled in for the night my baby
  and me
We switched 'round and 'round till half-
  past dawn
There was 57 channels and nothin' on

Well now home entertainment was my
  baby's wish
So I hopped into town for a satellite
  dish

I tied it to the top of my Japanese car
I came home and I pointed it out into
  the stars
A message came back from the great
  beyond
"There's 57 channels and nothin' on"

Well we might'a made some friends
  with some billionaires
We might'a got all nice and friendly
If we'd made it upstairs
All I got was a note that said "Bye-bye
  John
Our love is 57 channels and nothin' on"

So I bought a .44 Magnum, it was solid
  steel cast
And in the blessed name of Elvis, well I
  just let it blast
Till my TV lay in pieces there at my feet
And they busted me for disturbin' the
  almighty peace
Judge said "What you got in your
  defense, son?"
57 channels and nothin' on
I can see by your eyes, friend, you're
  just about gone
57 channels and nothin' on
57 channels and nothin' on

cross my heart

First time I crossed my heart
I was beggin' baby please
At your bedside down on my knees
When I crossed my heart
When I crossed my heart
I crossed my heart, pretty baby over you

Second time I crossed my heart
Rain came in from the south
I was lyin' there with something sweet
    and salty in my mouth
When I crossed my heart
When I crossed my heart
When I crossed my heart, pretty darlin'
    over you

Well you may think the world's black
    and white
And you're dirty or you're clean
You better watch out you don't slip
Through them spaces in between

Where the night gets sticky
And the sky gets black

I grabbed you, baby, you grabbed me
    back
And we crossed our hearts
We crossed our hearts
Yeah I crossed my heart

Little boys little girls
They know their wrongs from their
    rights
Once you cross your heart
We crossed our hearts
You ain't ever supposed to lie

Well life ain't nothin'
But a cold hard ride
I ain't leavin'
Till I'm satisfied
I cross my heart
Yeah I cross my heart
Well I cross my heart, pretty darlin'
    over you

gloria's eyes

I was your big man, I was your Prince
    Charming
King on a white horse, hey now look
    how far I've fallen
I tried to trick you, yeah, but baby you
    got wise
You cut me, cut me right down to size
Now I'm just a fool in Gloria's eyes

Swore I'd get you back I was so sure
I'd get you back like I done so many
    times before
A little sweet talk to cover over all of
    the lies
You came runnin' back but to my
    surprise
There was somethin' gone in Gloria's
    eyes

Well in the dark when it was just me
    and you

I asked the question that I knew the
    answer to
Is that a smile, my little dolly, on the
    shelf
Tell me is that a smile
Or is it somethin' else

Now I work hard to prove my love is
    true
Now I work hard and I bring it on home
    to you
At night I pray as silently you lie
Some day my love again will rise
Like a shining torch in Gloria's eyes

I was your big man, your Prince
    Charming
King on a white horse, now look how far
    I've fallen

with
every wish

Ol' catfish in the lake we called him
  Big Jim
When I was a kid my only wish was to
  get my line in him
Skipped church one Sunday, rowed out
  and throw'd in my line
Jim took that hook, pole and me right
  over the side
Went driftin' down past old tires and
  rusty cans of beer
The angel of the lake whispered in
  my ear
"Before you choose your wish, son
You better think first
With every wish there comes a curse"

I fell in love with beautiful Doreen
She was the prettiest thing this old
  town'd ever seen
I courted her and I made her mine
But I grew jealous whenever another
  man'd come walkin' down the line
And my jealousy made me treat her
  mean and cruel
She sighed "Bobby, oh Bobby, you're
  such a fool

Don't you know before you choose your
  wish
You'd better think first
'Cause with every wish there comes a
  curse"

These days I sit around and laugh
At the many rivers I've crossed
But on the far banks there's always
  another forest
Where a man can get lost
Well there in the high trees love's
  bluebird glides
Guiding us 'cross to another river on
  the other side
And there someone is waitin' with a
  look in her eyes
And though my heart's grown weary
And more than a little bit shy
Tonight I'll drink from her waters to
  quench my thirst
And leave the angels to worry
With every wish

Gloria's Eyes

Once I was a big man
darlin (baby) I was your prince charming
A king on a white horse

   oh baby how far I've fallen
I did something stupid, and baby you got wise
you cut me baby cut me right down
   to size now I'm just a fool
   in Gloria's eyes

in time   door
and I'd guess I smoothly talk you
and I'd win your heart back over like I'd so many
      times before
something was different [as the stars prophesized
  oh yea you gave in but soon I realized
(and soon yes you came back)
   something had changed + took the shine
      off my prize
for when I held you close I couldn't
   stand what I saw

and Gloria my love your words never revealed
what was it I saw I saw reflected
   in Gloria's

so now I work hard and baby I'll have to you
show will eyes darlin that I could do
    for you
I sweat + slave until once I claim my
   prize
   one day until once my love shall
   again I rise
  in Gloria's eyes

was shar a smile   shelf
was shar a smile or was it
         something else?

                         + swear your the only one
+ each night I caress you ~~runs~~ run my
figers thru your hair
searchy + searchy for   the light that's never   comes
            there butten
searchy in ~~vain~~ vain for the answer that

so I hold the question never comes
     so I'll sweat + slave until the day arrives
     when once again find/my love will rise
         in blue eyes

roll of the dice

Well I've been a losin' gambler
Just throwin' snake eyes
Love ain't got me downhearted
I know up around the corner lies
My fool's paradise
In just another roll of the dice

All my elevens and sevens been comin'
  up
Sixes and nines
But since I fell for you baby
Been comin' on changin' times
They're waitin' over the rise
Just another roll of the dice

I've stumbled and I know I made my
  mistakes
But tonight I'm gonna be playin' for all
  of the stakes

Well it's never too late, so come on girl

The tables are waiting
You and me and lady luck, well, tonight
We'll be celebrating
Drinkin' champagne on ice
In just another roll of the dice

High rollers lay down your bets and I'll
  raise 'em
Well I know the odds ain't in my favor

Maybe I'm just a clown throwin' down
Lookin' to come up busted
I'm a thief in the house of love
And I can't be trusted
Well I'll be makin' my heist
In just another roll of the dice
Just another roll of the dice
Move on up
Come on seven
Roll me baby
In this fool's heaven

real world

Mister Trouble come walkin' this way
Year gone past feels like one long day
But I'm alive and I'm feelin' all right
Well I run that hard road outta heart-
    break city
Built a roadside carnival out of hurt
    and self-pity
It was all wrong, well now I'm movin'
    on

Ain't no church bells ringing
Ain't no flags unfurled
Just me and you and the love we're
    bringing
Into the real world
Into the real world

I built a shrine in my heart, it wasn't
    pretty to see
Made out of fool's gold, memory and
    tears cried
Now I'm headin' over the rise
I'm searchin' for one clear moment of
    love and truth

I still got a little faith
But what I need is some proof tonight
I'm lookin' for it in your eyes

Ain't no church bells ringing
Ain't no flags unfurled
Just me and you and the love we're
    bringing
Into the real world
Into the real world

Well tonight I just wanna shout
I feel my soul waist deep and sinkin'
Into this black river of doubt
I just wanna rise and walk along the
    river side
And when the morning comes, baby, I
    don't wanna hide
I'll stand right at your side with my
    arms open wide

Well tonight I just wanna shout
I feel my soul waist deep and sinkin'
Into this black river of doubt

I just wanna rise and walk along the
    river side
Till the morning comes
I'll stand right by your side

I wanna find some answers, I wanna
    ask for some help
I'm tired of runnin' scared
Baby let's get our bags packed
We'll take it here to hell and heaven
    and back
And if love is hopeless, hopeless at best
Come on put on your party dress, it's
    ours tonight
And we're goin' with the tumblin' dice

Ain't no church bells ringing
Ain't no flags unfurled
Just me, you and the hope we're
    bringing
Into the real world
Well into the real world
Oh into the real world

all or
nothin' at all

Said you'd give me just a little kiss
And you'd rock me for a little while
Well you'd slip me just a piece of it
Listen up my little child
I want it all or nothin' at all
I want it all or nothin' at all

Said you'd take me for a little dance
If you had a little time on your hands
Well all I do is push and shove
Just to get a little piece of your love
I want it all or nothin' at all
I want it all or nothin' at all

Well now I don't wanna be greedy
But when it comes to love there ain't no
    doubt

You just ain't gonna get what you want
With one foot in bed and one foot out
You got to give it all or nothin' at all
All or nothin' at all

Now I only got a little time
So if you're gonna change your mind
Then shout out what you're thinkin' of
If what you're thinkin' of is love
I want it all or nothin' at all
I want it all or nothin' at all
I want to have it all or nothin' at all
I want it all or nothin' at all

I want it all or nothin' at all
I want to give it all or nothin' at all

man's job

Well you can go out with him
Play with all of his toys
But takin' care of you darlin'
Ain't for one of the boys
Oh there's somethin' in your soul
That he's gonna rob
And lovin' you baby, lovin' you darlin'
Lovin' you woman is a man's man's job

CHORUS:
Lovin' you is a man's job baby
Lovin' you is a man's job
Lovin' you is a man's job baby
Lovin' you is a man's job

Well now his kisses may thrill

Those other girls that he likes
But when it comes to treatin'
A real woman right
Well all of his tricks
No they won't be enough
'Cause lovin' you baby, lovin' you
   woman
Lovin' you darlin' is a man's man's job

(CHORUS)

You're dancin' with him, he's holding
   you tight
I'm standing here waitin' to catch your
   eye

Your hand's on his neck as the music
   sways
All my illusions slip away

Now if you're lookin' for a hero
Someone to save the day
Well darlin' my feet
They're made of clay
But I've got somethin' in my soul
And I wanna give it up
But gettin' up the nerve
Gettin' up the nerve
Gettin' up the nerve is a man's
   man's job

(CHORUS)

i wish i were blind

I love to see the cottonwood blossom
In the early spring
I love to see the message of love
That the bluebird brings
But when I see you walkin' with him
Down along the strand
I wish I were blind
When I see you with your man

I love to see your hair shining
In the long summer's light
I love to watch the stars fill the sky
On a summer night
The music plays, you take his hand
I watch how you touch him as you start
    to dance
And I wish I were blind

When I see you with your man

We struggle here but all our love's in
    vain
Oh these eyes that once filled me with
    your beauty
Now fill me with pain
And the light that once entered here
Is banished from me
And this darkness is all, baby, that my
    heart sees

And though this world is filled
With a grace and beauty of God's hand
Oh I wish I were blind
When I see you with your man

the long goodbye

My soul went walkin' but I stayed here
Feel like I been workin' for a thousand
  years
Chippin' away at this chain of my own
  lies
Climbin' a wall a hundred miles high
Well I woke up this morning on the
  other side
Yeah yeah this is the long goodbye
Hey yeah this is the long goodbye

Same old faces, it's the same old town
What once was laughs is draggin' me
  now
Waitin' on rain hangin' on for love
Words of forgiveness from some God
  above
Ain't no words of mercy comin' from on
  high
Oh no just a long goodbye

Well I went to leave twenty years ago
Since then I guess I been packin' kinda
  slow
Sure did like that admirin' touch
Guess I liked it a little too much

The moon is high and here I am
Sittin' here with this hammer in hand
One more drink oughtta ease the pain
Starin' at that last link in the chain
Well let's raise our glass and let the
  hammer fly
Hey yeah this is the long goodbye
Hey yeah this is the long goodbye
Kiss me baby and we're gonna fly
Hey yeah this is the long goodbye
Yeah yeah this is the long goodbye
Hey yeah this is the long goodbye
Kiss me baby 'cause we're gonna ride
Yeah yeah this is the long goodbye

real man

Took my baby to a picture show
Found a seat in the back row
Sound came up, lights went down
Rambo he was blowin' 'em down
I don't need no gun in my fist, baby
All I need is your sweet kiss
To get me feelin' like a real man
Feelin' like a real man
Well you can beat on your chest
Hell any monkey can
But you got me feelin' like a real man
Oh feelin' like a real man

Me and my girl Saturday night
Late movie on channel five
The girls were droppin', they're droppin'
    like flies

To some smooth-talkin' cool walkin'
    private eye
I ain't got no nerves of steel
But all I got to know is if your love
    is real
To get me feelin' like a real man
Oh feelin' like a real man
Well you can beat on your chest
Hell any monkey can
Your love's got me feelin' like a real
    man
Oh feelin' like a real man

I ain't no fighter, that's easy to see
And as a lover I ain't goin' down in
    history

But when the lights go down and you
    pull me close
Well I look in your eyes and there's one
    thing I know
Baby I'll be tough enough
If I can find the guts to give you all
    my love
Then I'll be feelin' like a real man
Feelin' like a real man
Well you can beat on your chest
Hell any monkey can
You got me feelin' like a real man
Oh feelin' like a real man
Yeah I been feelin' like a real man
Feelin' like a real man

lucky
town

The video shoot for "Better Days"

better days

Well my soul checked out missing as I
    sat listening
To the hours and minutes tickin' away
Yeah just sittin' around waitin' for my
    life to begin
While it was all just slippin' away
I'm tired of waitin' for tomorrow to
    come
Or that train to come roarin' 'round the
    bend
I got a new suit of clothes and a pretty
    red rose
And a woman I can call my friend

These are better days, baby
Yeah there's better days shining
    through
These are better days, baby
Better days with a girl like you

Well I took a piss at fortune's sweet kiss
It's like eatin' caviar and dirt
It's a sad funny ending to find yourself
    pretending
A rich man in a poor man's shirt
Now my ass was draggin' when from a
    passin' gypsy wagon
Your heart like a diamond shone
Tonight I'm layin' in your arms carvin'
    lucky charms
Out of these hard luck bones

These are better days, baby
These are better days it's true
These are better days, baby
There's better days shining through

Now a life of leisure and a pirate's
    treasure
Don't make much for tragedy

But it's a sad man, my friend, who's
    livin' in his own skin
And can't stand the company
Every fool's got a reason for feelin' sorry
    for himself
And turning his heart to stone
Tonight this fool's halfway to heaven
    and just a mile outta hell
And I feel like I'm comin' home

These are better days, baby
There's better days shining through
These are better days
Better days with a girl like you

These are better days, baby
These are better days it's true
These are better days
Better days are shining through

lucky town

House got too crowded, clothes got too
tight
And I don't know just where I'm going
tonight
Out where the sky's been cleared by a
good hard rain
There's somebody callin' my secret
name

I'm going down to Lucky Town
Going down to Lucky Town
I wanna lose these blues I've found
Down in Lucky Town
Down in Lucky Town

Had a coat of fine leather and snake-
skin boots
But that coat always had a thread
hangin' loose
Well I pulled it one night and to my
surprise
It led me right past your house and on
over the rise

I'm going down to Lucky Town
Down to Lucky Town

I wanna lose these blues I've found
Down in Lucky Town
Down in Lucky Town

I had some victory that was just failure
in deceit
Now the joke's comin' up through the
soles of my feet
I been a long time walking on fortune's
cane
Tonight I'm steppin' lightly and feelin'
no pain

Well here's to your good looks, baby,
now here's to my health
Here's to the loaded places that we take
ourselves
When it comes to luck you make your
own
Tonight I got dirt on my hands but I'm
building me a new home

Down in Lucky Town
Down in Lucky Town
I'm gonna lose these blues I've found
Down in Lucky Town

With good friend and road buddy Matt Delia on Route 66, Arizona

local hero

I was driving through my hometown
I was just kinda killin' time
When I seen a face staring out of a
   black velvet painting
From the window of the five-and-dime
I couldn't quite recall the name
But the pose looked familiar to me
So I asked the salesgirl "Who was that
   man
Between the Doberman and Bruce Lee?"
She said "Just a local hero
Local hero" she said with a smile
"Yeah a local hero
He used to live here for a while"

I met a stranger dressed in black
At the train station
He said "Son your soul can be saved"
There's beautiful women, nights of low
   livin'

And some dangerous money to be made
There's a big town 'cross the whiskey
   line
And if we turn the right cards up
They make us boss, the devil pays off
And them folks that are real hard up
They get their local hero
Somebody with the right style
They get their local hero
Somebody with just the right smile

Well I learned my job, I learned it well
Fit myself with religion and a story to
   tell
First they made me the king, then they
   made me pope
Then they brought the rope

I woke to a gypsy girl sayin' "Drink this"

Well my hands had lost all sensation
These days I'm feeling all right
'Cept I can't tell my courage from my
   desperation
From the tainted chalice
Well I drunk some heady wine
Tonight I'm layin' here
But there's something in my ear
Sayin' there's a little town just beneath
   the floodline
Needs a local hero
Somebody with the right style
Lookin' for a local hero
Somebody with the right smile
"Local hero, local hero" she said with a
   smile
Local hero, he used to live here for a
   while

Overleaf: With the hardest-working dog in show business. *Lucky Town* photo shoot.

if i should
fall behind

We said we'd walk together, baby come
   what may
That come the twilight should we lose
   our way
If as we're walking a hand should slip
   free
I'll wait for you
And if I should fall behind
Wait for me

We swore we'd travel, darlin' side by
   side
We'd help each other stay in stride
But each lover's steps fall so differently
But I'll wait for you
And if I should fall behind
Wait for me

Now everyone dreams of a love lasting
   and true

But you and I know what this world
   can do
So let's make our steps clear that the
   other may see
And I'll wait for you
If I should fall behind
Wait for me

Now there's a beautiful river in the
   valley ahead
There 'neath the oak's bough soon we
   will be wed
Should we lose each other in the
   shadow of the evening trees
I'll wait for you
And should I fall behind
Wait for me
Darlin' I'll wait for you
Should I fall behind
Wait for me

leap of faith

All over the world the rain was pourin'
I was scratchin' where it itched
Oh heartbreak and despair got nothing
   but boring
So I grabbed you baby like a wild pitch

CHORUS:
It takes a leap of faith to get things
   going
It takes a leap of faith, you gotta show
   some guts
It takes a leap of faith to get things
   going
In your heart you must trust

Now your legs were heaven, your
   breasts were the altar
Your body was the holy land
You shouted "jump" but my heart
   faltered
You laughed and said "Baby don't you
   understand?"

(CHORUS)

Now you were the Red Sea, I was Moses
I kissed you and slipped into a bed of
   roses

The waters parted and love rushed
   inside
I was Jesus' son sanctified

Tonight the moon's looking young but
   I'm feelin' younger
'Neath a veil of dreams sweet blessings
   rain
Honey I can feel the first breeze of
   summer
And in your love I'm born again

(CHORUS)

the big
muddy

Billy had a mistress down on A and
   Twolfth
She was that little somethin' that he did
   for himself
His own little secret didn't hurt nobody
Come the afternoon he'd take her wadin'

CHORUS:
Waist deep in the big muddy
Waist deep in the big muddy
You start out standing but end up
   crawlin'

Got in some trouble and needed a hand
   from a friend of mine
This old friend he had a figure in mind
It was nothing illegal, just a little bit
   funny
He said "C'mon don't tell me that the
   rich don't know
Sooner or later it all comes down to
   money"
And you're waist deep in the big muddy

Waist deep in the big muddy
You start on higher ground but end up
   crawlin'

Well I had a friend said "You watch
   what you do
Poison snake bites you and you're
   poison too"

How beautiful the river flows and the
   birds they sing
But you and I we're messier things
There ain't no one leavin' this world,
   buddy
Without their shirttail dirty or their
   hands bloody

Waist deep in the big muddy
Waist deep in the big muddy
You start on higher ground but end up
   somehow crawlin'
Waist deep in the big muddy

living proof

Well now on a summer night in a dusky
 room
Come a little piece of the Lord's undying
 light
Crying like he swallowed the fiery moon
In his mother's arms it was all the
 beauty I could take
Like the mission words to some prayer
 that I could never make
In a world so hard and dirty, so fouled
 and confused
Searching for a little bit of God's mercy
I found living proof

I put my heart and soul, I put 'em high
 up on a shelf
Right next to the faith, the faith that I'd
 lost in myself

I went down into the desert city
Just tryin' so hard to shed my skin
I crawled deep into some kind of
 darkness
Lookin' to burn out every trace of who
 I'd been
You do some sad sad things, baby
When it's you you're tryin' to lose
You do some sad and hurtful things
I've seen living proof

You shot through my anger and rage
To show me my prison was just an open
 cage
There were no keys, no guards
Just one frightened man and some old
 shadows for bars

Well now all that's sure on the
 boulevard
Is that life is just a house of cards
As fragile as each and every breath
Of this boy sleepin' in our bed
Tonight let's lie beneath the eaves
Just a close band of happy thieves
And when that train comes we'll get on
 board
And steal what we can from the
 treasures, treasures of the Lord
It's been a long long drought, baby
Tonight the rain's pourin' down on
 our roof
Looking for a little bit of God's mercy
I found living proof

book of
dreams

I'm standing in the backyard
Listening to the party inside
Tonight I'm drinkin' in the forgiveness
This life provides
The scars we carry remain but the pain
   slips away it seems
Oh won't you, baby, be in my book of
   dreams

I'm watchin' you through the window
With your girlfriends from back home
You're showin' off your dress
There's laughter and a toast
From your daddy to the prettiest bride
   he's ever seen
Oh won't you, baby, be in my book of
   dreams

In the darkness my fingers slip across
   your skin

I feel your sweet reply
The room fades away and suddenly I'm
   way up high
Just holdin' you to me
As through the window the moonlight
   streams
Oh won't you, baby, be in my book of
   dreams

Now the ritual begins
'Neath the wedding garland we meet as
   strangers
The dance floor is alive with beauty
Mystery and danger
We dance out 'neath the stars' ancient
   light into the darkening trees
Oh won't you, baby, be in my book of
   dreams

souls of the departed

On the road to Basra stood young
    Lieutenant Jimmy Bly
Detailed to go through the clothes of
    the soldiers who died
At night in dreams he sees their souls
    rise
Like dark geese into the Oklahoma skies

Well this is a prayer for the souls of the
    departed
Those who've gone and left their babies
    brokenhearted
This is a prayer for the souls of the
    departed

Now Raphael Rodriquez was just seven
    years old
Shot down in a schoolyard by some East
    Compton *cholos*
His mama cried "My beautiful boy is
    dead"
In the hills the self-made men just
    sighed and shook their heads

This is a prayer for the souls of the
    departed
Those who've gone and left their babies
    brokenhearted
Young lives over before they got started
This is a prayer for the souls of the
    departed

Tonight as I tuck my own son in bed
All I can think of is what if it would've
    been him instead
I want to build me a wall so high
    nothing can burn it down
Right here on my own piece of dirty
    ground

Now I ply my trade in the land of king
    dollar
Where you get paid and your silence
    passes as honor
And all the hatred and dirty little lies
Been written off the books and into
    decent men's eyes

my beautiful reward

Well I sought gold and diamond rings
My own drug to ease the pain that
   living brings
Walked from the mountain to the valley
   floor
Searching for my beautiful reward
Searching for my beautiful reward

From a house on a hill a sacred light
   shines
I walk through these rooms but none of
   them are mine
Down empty hallways I went from door
   to door
Searching for my beautiful reward
Searching for my beautiful reward

Well your hair shone in the sun
I was so high I was the lucky one
Then I came crashing down like a drunk
   on a barroom floor
Searching for my beautiful reward
Searching for my beautiful reward

Tonight I can feel the cold wind at my
   back
I'm flyin' high over gray fields, my
   feathers long and black
Down along the river's silent edge I soar
Searching for my beautiful reward
Searching for my beautiful reward

from greatest hits

streets of philadelphia

secret garden

murder incorporated

blood brothers

this hard land

One afternoon in 1994 I received a phone call from Jonathan Demme. We'd met a few years earlier on a video shoot. Jonathan was calling to ask if I'd consider writing a song for a film he was currently directing called *Philadelphia.* The film was about a gay man's battle with AIDS and the fight to retain his position at a prestigious Philadelphia law firm.

I had my studio set up at home in Rumson and for a few afternoons I went in with some lyrics I had partially written dealing with the death of a close friend. Jonathan requested a rock song to open the film. I spent a day or so trying to accommodate, but the lyrics I had seemed to resist being put to rock music. So I began to fiddle with the synthesizer, playing over a hip-hop-influenced beat I programmed on the drum machine. As soon as I slowed the rhythm down over some basic minor

streets of philadelphia

I was bruised and battered and I
    couldn't tell what I felt
I was unrecognizable to myself
I saw my reflection in a window
I didn't know my own face
Oh brother are you gonna leave me
    wastin' away
On the streets of Philadelphia

I walked the avenue till my legs felt like
    stone
I heard the voices of friends vanished
    and gone
At night I could hear the blood in my
    veins
Black and whispering as the rain

On the streets of Philadelphia

Ain't no angel gonna greet me
It's just you and I, my friend
My clothes don't fit me no more
I walked a thousand miles
Just to slip this skin

The night has fallen, I'm lyin' awake
I can feel myself fading away
So receive me, brother, with your
    faithless kiss
Or will we leave each other alone like
    this
On the streets of Philadelphia

secret garden

She'll let you in her house
If you come knockin' late at night
She'll let you in her mouth
If the words you say are right
If you pay the price
She'll let you deep inside
But there's a secret garden she hides

She'll let you in her car
To go drivin' 'round
She'll let you into the parts of herself
That'll bring you down
She'll let you in her heart
If you got a hammer and a vise
But into her secret garden, don't think
     twice

You've gone a million miles
How far'd you get
To that place where you can't remember
And you can't forget

She'll lead you down a path
There'll be tenderness in the air
She'll let you come just far enough
So you know she's really there
She'll look at you and smile
And her eyes will say
She's got a secret garden
Where everything you want
Where everything you need
Will always stay
A million miles away

murder incorporated

Bobby's got a gun that he keeps
  beneath his pillow
Out on the street your chances are zero
Take a look around you (come on now)
It ain't too complicated
You're messin' with Murder
  Incorporated

Now you check over your shoulder
  everywhere that you go
Walkin' down the street there's eyes in
  every shadow
You better take a look around you (come
  on now)
That equipment you got's so outdated
You can't compete with Murder
  Incorporated
Everywhere you look now, Murder
  Incorporated

So you keep a little secret deep down
  inside your dresser drawer
For dealing with the heat you're feelin'
  out on the killin' floor

No matter where you step you feel
  you're never out of danger
So the comfort that you keep's a gold-
  plated snub-nose .32
I heard that you
Got a job downtown man that leaves
  your head cold
Everywhere you look life's ain't got
  no soul
That apartment you live in feels like it's
  just a place to hide
When you're walkin' down the street you
  won't meet no one eye to eye
The cops reported you as just another
  homicide
But I can tell that you were just
  frustrated
From living with Murder Incorporated
Everywhere you look now, Murder
  Incorporated
Murder Incorporated

blood brothers

We played the King of the Mountain out
  on the end
The world came chargin' up the hill and
  we were women and men
Now there's so much that time, time
  and memory fade away
We got our own roads to ride and
  chances we gotta take
We stood side by side each one fightin'
  for the other
We said until we died we'd always be
  blood brothers

Now the hardness of this world slowly
  grinds your dreams away
Makin' a fool's joke out of the promises
  we make
And what once seemed black and white
  turns to so many shades of gray
We lose ourselves in work to do and
  bills to pay
And it's a ride, ride, ride, and there
  ain't much cover

With no one runnin' by your side, my
  blood brother

On through the houses of the dead past
  those fallen in their tracks
Always movin' ahead and never lookin'
  back
Now I don't know how I feel, I don't
  know how I feel tonight
If I've fallen 'neath the wheel, if I've
  lost or I've gained sight
I don't even know why, I don't know why
  I made this call
Or if any of this matters anymore
  after all

But the stars are burnin' bright like
  some mystery uncovered
I'll keep movin' through the dark with
  you in my heart
My blood brother

this hard land

Hey there mister can you tell me what
   happened to the seeds I've sown
Can you give me a reason, sir, as to
   why they've never grown
They've just blown around from town to
   town
Till they're back out on these fields
Where they fall from my hand
Back into the dirt of this hard land

Now me and my sister from German-
   town
We did ride
We made our bed, sir, from the rock on
   the mountainside
We been blowin' around from town to
   town
Lookin' for a place to stand
Where the sun burst through the cloud
To fall like a circle
Like a circle of fire down on this hard
   land

Now even the rain it don't come 'round
It don't come 'round here no more
And the only sound at night's the wind
Slammin' the back porch door
It just stirs you up like it wants to blow
   you down
Twistin' and churnin' up the sand
Leavin' all them scarecrows lyin' face-
   down
Facedown in the dirt of this hard land

From a building up on the hill
I can hear a tape deck blastin' "Home
   on the Range"
I can see them Bar-M choppers
Sweepin' low across the plains
It's me and you, Frank, we're lookin' for
   lost cattle
Our hooves twistin' and churnin' up the
   sand

We're ridin' in the whirlwind searchin'
   for lost treasure
Way down south of the Rio Grande
We're ridin' 'cross that river
In the moonlight
Up onto the banks of this hard land

Hey, Frank, won't you pack your bags
And meet me tonight down at Liberty
   Hall
Just one kiss from you, my brother
And we'll ride until we fall
We'll sleep in the fields
We'll sleep by the rivers and in the
   morning
We'll make a plan
Well if you can't make it
Stay hard, stay hungry, stay alive
If you can
And meet me in a dream of this hard
   land

the ghost of tom joad

Recording *Tom Joad* in California

The Ghost of Tom Joad" was among the songs I wrote for the E Street Band to complete the *Greatest Hits* album. It started out as a rock song. But it didn't feel right, so I set it aside. I returned to it some months later, while still unsure of what I wanted to work on next. After working with the band in New York, I went back to California and started recording at home. I had

"Straight Time," "Highway 29," and "The Ghost of Tom Joad." I also had a notebook filled with unfinished song ideas.

I began recording with just myself and my acoustic guitar. When I felt I had some workable material, I put together a small, five-piece group. Once I cut "Tom Joad," I had a feeling for the record I wanted to make. It was an acoustic album where I picked up elements of the themes I

273

had worked on in the past and set the stories in the mid-'90s.

As with *Nebraska,* on "Tom Joad" and the songs that followed, the music was minimal; the melodies were uncomplicated, yet played an important role in the storytelling process. The simplicity and plainness, the austere rhythms defined who these characters were and how they expressed themselves.

The precision of the storytelling in these types of songs is very important. The correct detail can speak volumes about who your character is, while the wrong one can shred the credibility of your story. When you get the music and lyrics right in these songs, your voice disappears into the voices of those you've chosen to write about. Basically, I find the characters and listen to them. That always leads to a series of questions about their behavior: What would they do? What would they never do? You try to locate the rhythm of their speech and the nature of their expression.

But all the telling detail in the world doesn't matter if the song lacks an emotional center. That's something you have to pull out of yourself from the commonality you feel with the man or woman you're writing about. By pulling these elements together as well as you can, you shed light on their lives and respect their experiences.

On *Tom Joad* one song led to another. The ex-con of "Straight Time" became the shoe salesman of "Highway 29." The unemployed steelworker of "Youngstown" left the Monongahela Valley and became "The New Timer." These last two songs, along with "The Ghost of Tom Joad," chronicled the increasing economic division of the '80s and '90s and the hard times and consequences for many of the people whose work and sacrifice helped build the country we live in.

With tour director George Travis

A lot of the songs on *The Ghost of Tom Joad* have settings in the Southwest. I'd been through the Central Valley many times on the way to visiting my parents. I'd often stop and spend some time in the small farm towns off the interstate. But it still took a good amount of research to get the details of the region correct. I traced the stories out slowly and carefully. I thought hard about who these people were and the choices they were presented with.

In California there was a sense of a new country being formed on the edge of the old. But the old stories of race and exclusion continued to be played out. I tried to catch a small piece of this on the songs I wrote for *Tom Joad*. "Sinaloa Cowboys," "The Line," "Balboa Park," and "Across the Border" were songs that traced the lineage of my earlier characters to the Mexican migrant experience in the New West. These songs completed a circle, bringing me back to 1978 and the inspiration I'd gotten from Steinbeck's *The Grapes of Wrath*. Their skin was darker and their language had changed, but these were people trapped by the same brutal circumstances.

By the end of *Tom Joad,* I'd written about the death and personal destruction that accompany the lives of many of the people who inspired these songs. I was working on "Galveston Bay," a song that originally had a more violent ending. But it began to feel false. If I was going to find some small window of light, I had to do it with this man in this song.

I had already written "Across the Border," a song that was like a prayer or dream you have the night before you're going to take a dangerous journey. The singer seeks a home where his love will be rewarded, his faith restored, where a tenuous peace and hope may exist. With "Galveston Bay" I had to make these ideas feel attainable. The song asks the question, Is the most political act an individual one, something that happens in the dark, in the quiet, when someone makes a particular decision that affects his immediate world? I wanted a character who is driven to do the wrong thing, but does not. He instinctively refuses to add to the violence in the world around him. With great difficulty and against his own grain he transcends his circumstances. He finds the strength and grace to save himself and the part of the world he touches.

The album ends with "My Best Was Never Good Enough," which was inspired by the cliché-popping sheriff in noir writer Jim Thompson's book *The Killer Inside Me.* It was my parting joke and shot at the way pop culture trivializes complicated moral issues, how the nightly news "sound bytes" and packages life to strip away the dignity of human events.

I knew that *The Ghost of Tom Joad* wouldn't attract my largest audience. But I was sure the songs on it added up to a reaffirmation of the best of what I do. The record was something new, but it was also a reference point to the things I tried to stand for and be about as a songwriter.

the ghost
of tom joad

Men walkin' 'long the railroad tracks
Goin' someplace there's no goin' back
Highway patrol choppers comin' up over
  the ridge
Hot soup on a campfire under the
  bridge

Shelter line stretchin' 'round the corner
Welcome to the new world order
Families sleepin' in their cars in the
  Southwest
No home, no job, no peace, no rest

The highway is alive tonight
But nobody's kiddin' nobody about
  where it goes
I'm sittin' down here in the campfire
  light
Searchin' for the ghost of Tom Joad

He pulls a prayer book out of his
  sleeping bag
Preacher lights up a butt and takes
  a drag
Waitin' for when the last shall be first
  and the first shall be last
In a cardboard box 'neath the under-
  pass

Got a one-way ticket to the promised
  land

You got a hole in your belly and a gun
  in your hand
Sleeping on a pillow of solid rock
Bathin' in the city aqueduct

The highway is alive tonight
Where it's headed everybody knows
I'm sittin' down here in the campfire
  light
Waitin' on the ghost of Tom Joad

Now Tom said "Mom, wherever there's a
  cop beatin' a guy
Wherever a hungry newborn baby cries
Where there's a fight 'gainst the blood
  and hatred in the air
Look for me, Mom, I'll be there
Wherever there's somebody fightin' for a
  place to stand
Or decent job or a helpin' hand
Wherever somebody's strugglin' to be
  free
Look in their eyes, Mom, you'll see me"

Well the highway is alive tonight
But nobody's kiddin' nobody about
  where it goes
I'm sittin' down here in the campfire
  light
With the ghost of old Tom Joad

straight time .

Got out of prison back in '86 and I
    found a wife
Walked the clean and narrow
Just tryin' to stay out and stay alive
Got a job at the rendering plant, it ain't
    gonna make me rich
In the darkness before dinner comes
Sometimes I can feel the itch
I got a cold mind to go tripping 'cross
    that thin line
I'm sick of doin' straight time

My uncle's at the evenin' table, makes
    his living runnin' hot cars
Slips me a hundred-dollar bill says
"Charlie you best remember who your
    friends are"
Got a cold mind to go tripping 'cross
    that thin line
I ain't makin' straight time

Eight years in it feels like you're gonna
    die

But you get used to anything
Sooner or later it just becomes your life

Kitchen floor in the evening tossin' my
    little babies high
Mary's smiling but she's watching me
    out of the corner of her eye
Seems you can't get any more than
    half free
I step out onto the front porch and suck
    the cold air deep inside of me
Got a cold mind to go tripping 'cross
    that thin line
I'm sick of doin' straight time

In the basement, huntin' gun and a
    hacksaw
Sip a beer and thirteen inches of barrel
    drop to the floor
Come home in the evening, can't get
    the smell from my hands
Lay my head down on the pillow
And go driftin' off into foreign lands

h i g h w a y   2 9

I slipped on her shoe, she was a perfect
   size seven
I said "There's no smokin' in the store,
   ma'am"
She crossed her legs and then
We made some small talk, that's where
   it should have stopped
She slipped me her number, I put it in
   my pocket
My hand slipped up her skirt, every-
   thing slipped my mind
In that little roadhouse
On Highway 29

It was a small-town bank, it was a
   mess
Well I had a gun, you know the rest
Money on the floorboards, shirt was
   covered in blood
And she was cryin', her and me we
   headed south
On Highway 29

In a little desert motel the air was hot
   and clean
I slept the sleep of the dead, I didn't
   dream

I woke in the morning, washed my face
   in the sink
We headed into the Sierra Madres
   'cross the border line
The winter sun shot through the black
   trees
I told myself it was all something in her
But as we drove I knew it was some-
   thing in me
Something that'd been comin' for a
   long long time
And something that was here with me
   now
On Highway 29

The road was filled with broken glass
   and gasoline
She wasn't sayin' nothin', it was just a
   dream
The wind come silent through the wind-
   shield
All I could see was snow, sky and pines
I closed my eyes and I was runnin'
I was runnin', then I was flyin'

t was spring of '98. The E Street Band was about to embark on its first world tour in eighteen years. As I stood on our rehearsal stage at Convention Hall in Asbury Park, I was confident the band was playing well. We had our show. However, I felt I needed one new song that would set us firmly down in the present. Something that would reaffirm our sense of purpose and capture our current ambitions, that would let our fans know once again what we were here for.

The band has always given me confidence to tackle large themes. Something about the size and sound of the music we make, the depth of the relationships, brings this out in my writing. They give me courage. As a group, we're old school, mechanical, tactile, hot not cool, we run on fire not ice. During rehearsals the image of the band as this big train coming down the track, rolling into your town, smokestacks blowin', kept recurring to me.

In my notebook I had an unfinished song, "Land of Hope and Dreams." "Grab your ticket and your suitcase/Thunder's rolling down the track/I don't know where we're goin' . . . /Big wheels roll through fields where sunlight streams. . . ."

Most of my songs are set on the near banks of the river, in *this* world, where we all have to make our way. They tally up the costs to make a life on these banks. The struggle, the fight. "Land of Hope and Dreams" had its sights set on the "far shore" in the land of promise and peace where "faith shall be rewarded."

I played with the refrain from "This Train," the old folk spiritual. Instead of a chorus of exclusion, "This train *don't* carry no gamblers," I wanted my refrain to be inclusive: "This train carries . . ." everybody.

As we worked this chorus up in the final days of rehearsal with Steve, Patti, Nils, and Clarence singing a gospel harmony and the band rocking underneath, I could feel its rolling power. The first night we closed the show with it; by the second night the crowd was singing it back to us.

land of hope and dreams

Grab your ticket and your suitcase
Thunder's rollin' down this track
You don't know where you're goin'
But you know you won't be back
Darlin' if you're weary
Lay your head upon my chest
We'll take what we can carry
And we'll leave the rest

Big wheels roll through fields where
Sunlight streams
Meet me in a
Land of hope and dreams

I will provide for you
And I'll stand by your side
You'll need a good companion for
This part of the ride
Leave behind your sorrows
Let this day be the last

Tomorrow there'll be sunshine
And all this darkness past

Big wheels roll through fields where
Sunlight streams
Meet me in a
Land of hope and dreams

This train . . .
Carries saints and sinners
This train . . .
Carries losers and winners
This train . . .
Carries whores and gamblers
This train . . .
Carries lost souls
This train . . .
Dreams will not be thwarted
This train . . .
Faith will be rewarded
This train . . .

Hear the steel wheels singin'
This train . . . .
Bells of freedom ringin'

This train . . .
Carries broken-hearted
This train . . .
Thieves and sweet souls departed
This train . . .
Carries fools and kings
This train . . .
All aboard

This train . . .
Dreams will not be thwarted
This train . . .
Faith will be rewarded
This train . . .
Hear the steel wheels singin'
This train . . .
Bells of freedom ringin'

had the title "American Skin" and a few stray lines, an idea for a song about American identity, sitting in my workbook for six months. In the weeks leading up to our New York shows, the tour's finale, I'd been thinking about the case of Amadou Diallo, the innocent African immigrant gunned down in a tragic accident by undercover police detectives outside his apartment in New York City. He'd been shot 41 times. The sheer number of shots seemed to gauge the size of our betrayal of one another. "41 shots . . . 41 shots," that was the mantra I wanted to repeat over and over throughout my song, the daily compounding of crimes—large and small—against one another.

Though the song was critical, it was not "anti-police" as some thought. The first voice you hear after the intro is from the policeman's point of view: "Kneeling over his body in the vestibule praying for his life." In the second verse, a mother tries to impress upon her young son the importance of his simplest actions in a neighborhood where the most innocent of motions (your hand reaching for your wallet, or not in sight) can be misinterpreted with deadly consequences.

In the bridge, the verses "Is it in your heart, is it in your eyes" asks the singer and his audience to look inside themselves for their own collaboration in events. In the third verse we're "baptized in these waters and in each other's blood . . . It ain't no secret/No secret my friend/You can get killed just for living/In your American skin." Life in the land of brotherly fear.

We debuted "American Skin" in Atlanta a few nights before we hit New York, and the audience responded powerfully. By the time we got to New York City, we were the talk of the tabloids. We were attacked in the newspapers, and I received letters from officials asking me not to play the song. If the people hadn't been serious about what they were writing (a song that very few people had even heard yet), a lot of it would have been funny.

I worked hard for a balanced voice. I knew a diatribe would do no good. I just wanted to help people see the other guy's point of view. The idea was here: Here is what systematic racial injustice, fear, and paranoia do to our children, our loved ones, ourselves. Here is the price in blood.

The air was thick in the Garden that night. The band gathered in the back a few feet from the stage as the house lights came down. We put our hands together as we often do before a show. I said, "This is what we were built for, let's go!"

american skin
[41 shots]

41 shots . . . and we'll take that ride
'Cross this bloody river
To the other side
41 shots . . . cut through the night
You're kneeling over his body in the vestibule
Praying for his life

Is it a gun, is it a knife
Is it a wallet, this is your life
It ain't no secret
It ain't no secret
No secret my friend
You can get killed just for living
In your American skin

41 shots . . . Lena gets her son ready for school
She says "On these streets, Charles
You've got to understand the rules
If an officer stops you
Promise me you'll always be polite, that you'll never
     ever run away
Promise Mama you'll keep your hands in sight"

Is it a gun, is it a knife
Is it a wallet, this is your life

It ain't no secret
It ain't no secret
No secret my friend
You can get killed just for living
In your American skin

Is it a gun, is it a knife
Is it in your heart, is it in your eyes
It ain't no secret . . .

41 shots . . . and we'll take that ride
'Cross this bloody river
To the other side
41 shots . . . got my boots caked in this mud
We're baptized in these waters and in each
     other's blood

Is it a gun, is it a knife
Is it a wallet, this is your life
It ain't no secret
It ain't no secret
No secret my friend
You can get killed just for living
In your American skin

the rising

fter 132 shows on the road, the band was in good form. "Land of Hope and Dreams" and "American Skin" gave me the confidence that I could still write the music we delivered well, that we could take the original idea and philosophy of the band and develop it into the present. Now it was time to make a record . . . with the E Street Band.

In the fall of 2000, we organized a weekend of sessions in New York City. We cut some songs I had been holding on to for a while for an impending rock record. The work went smoothly, but later, on repeated listening, something was missing. We were going to need some new material and a different approach to production. A few years earlier, Sony President Donnie Ienner had said that Brendan O'Brien, producer of Pearl Jam and Rage Against the Machine, mentioned that he would be interested in working with me. Our usual glacial pace took its course, so here we were years later calling to arrange a meeting. Shortly thereafter, Brendan and I got together in my home stu-

dio in New Jersey. I played him some old demos, which included "Nothing Man," "Further On," and the take of "My City of Ruins" I had cut with the band the preceding fall. We got on well and decided we'd get together in a month or so and cut a couple of songs down in Atlanta at Southern Tracks Studios, where Brendan works regularly.

The Rising had its origins in the national telethon we were invited to be a part of the week after September 11. I wrote "Into the Fire" for that show (it remained incomplete, so I performed "My City of Ruins," the song I had written a year earlier for Asbury Park). Of the many tragic images of that day, the picture I couldn't let go of was of the emergency workers going up the stairs as others rushed down to safety. The sense of duty, the courage. Ascending into . . . what? The religious image of ascension. The crossing of the line between this world, the world of blood, work, family, your children, earth, the breath in your lungs, the ground beneath your feet. All that is this life and

. . . the next. If you love life or any part of it, the depth of their sacrifice was unthinkable and incomprehensible. Yet what they left behind was shortly to become very tangible. Death, along with all its anger, its pain and loss, opens a window of possibility for the living. It removes the veil that the "ordinary" gently drapes over our eyes. Renewed sight is the hero's last loving gift to those left behind.

The telethon seemed a way to give thanks for community protected and preserved, to the people and their families who take that burden on as a part of their everyday lives.

"Into the Fire" was a folk-blues with a gospel chorus, the grittiness and sacrifice of the blues giving the gospel elements "may your strength give us strength . . ." their meaning. "Into the Fire" unlocked the rest of the record. Occasionally, you'll write something that will guide you through the story you are about to tell. Everything else you write falls in relation to this key element, this key song. This was how *The Rising* developed. "You're Missing" came next, the daily details of loss, the unrequited waiting, the incompleteness.

These were the two songs we cut when I went to Atlanta. Brendan brought a fresh power and focus to the band's sound and playing. After a few days he said, "These are good, now go home and write some more." I went home, searched my book for unfinished songs, and continued to write. "Waitin' On a Sunny Day" was a song I'd had for a year or so that found its place within this new material. We recut "Nothing Man," a song I'd had since '94. It captured the awkwardness and isolation of survival. "I don't remember how I felt . . . I never thought I'd live. . . ." "Countin' On a Miracle" was new . . . hope in vain, still waiting on, insisting on life . . . insisting on your own life. "Empty Sky" was the last song I wrote. My art director sent me a photo of clouds in an empty sky,

countin' on a miracle

It's a fairytale so tragic
There's no prince to break the spell
I don't believe in magic
But for you I will, for you I will
If I'm a fool, I'll be a fool
Darlin' for you

CHORUS:
I'm countin' on a miracle
Baby I'm countin' on a miracle
Darlin' I'm countin' on a miracle
To come through

There ain't no storybook story
There's no never-ending song
Our happily ever after, Darlin'
Forever come and gone
I'm movin' on
If I'm gonna believe

I'll put my faith
Darlin' in you

I'm countin' on a miracle
Baby I'm countin' on a miracle
Darlin' I'm countin' on a miracle
To come through

Sleeping beauty awakes from her
    dream
With her lover's kiss on her lips
Your kiss was taken from me
Now all I have is this . . .

Your kiss, your kiss, your touch, your
    touch
Your heart, your heart, your strength,
    your strength
Your hope, your hope, your faith, your
    faith

Your face, your face, your love, your love
Your dream, your dream, your life, your
    life

I'm runnin' through the forest
With the wolf at my heels
My king is lost at midnight
When the tower bells peal
We've got no fairytale ending
In God's hands our fate is complete
Your heaven's here in my heart
Our love's this dust beneath my feet
Just this dust beneath my feet
If I'm gonna live
I'll lift my life
Darlin' to you

(CHORUS)

empty sky

I woke up this morning
I could barely breathe
Just an empty impression
In the bed where you used to be
I want a kiss from your lips
I want an eye for an eye
I woke up this morning to an empty sky

Empty sky, empty sky
I woke up this morning to an empty sky
Empty sky, empty sky
I woke up this morning to an empty sky

Blood on the streets
Blood flowin' down
I hear the blood of my blood
Cryin' from the ground

Empty sky, empty sky
I woke up this morning to the empty sky

Empty sky, empty sky
I woke up this morning to the empty sky

On the plains of Jordan
I cut my bow from the wood
Of this tree of evil
Of this tree of good
I want a kiss from your lips
I want an eye for an eye
I woke up this morning to the empty sky

Empty sky, empty sky
I woke up this morning to an empty sky
Empty sky, empty sky
I woke up this morning to the empty sky
Empty sky, empty sky
I woke up this morning to an empty sky

the fuse

Down at the court house they're ringin'
   the flag down
Long black line of cars snakin' slow
   through town
Red sheets snappin' on the line
With this ring, will you be mine
The fuse is burning
(Shut out the lights)
The fuse is burning
(Come on let me do you right)

Trees on fire with the first fall's frost
Long black line in front of Holy Cross
Blood moon risin' in a sky of black dust
Tell me Baby who do you trust?
The fuse is burning
(Shut out the lights)
The fuse is burning
(Come on let me do you right)

Tires on the highway hissin' something's
   coming
You can feel the wires in the tree tops
   hummin'
Devil's on the horizon line
Your kiss and I'm alive

A quiet afternoon, an empty house
On the edge of the bed you slip off your
   blouse
The room is burning with the noon sun
Your bittersweet taste on my tongue

The fuse is burning
(Shut out the lights)
The fuse is burning
(Come on let me do you right)

mary's place

I got seven pictures of Buddha
The prophet's on my tongue
Eleven angels of mercy
Sighin' over that black hole in the sun
My heart's dark but it's risin'
I'm pullin' all the faith I can see
From that black hole on the horizon
I hear your voice calling me

Let it rain, let it rain, let it rain
Let it rain, let it rain, let it rain, let it
  rain
Meet me at Mary's place, we're gonna
  have a party
Meet me at Mary's place, we're gonna
  have a party
Tell me how do we get this thing started
Meet me at Mary's place

Familiar faces around me
Laughter fills the air
Your loving grace surrounds me
Everybody's here
Furniture's out on the front porch
Music's up loud
I dream of you in my arms
I lose myself in the crowd

Let it rain, let it rain, let it rain
Let it rain, let it rain, let it rain, let it
  rain
Meet me at Mary's place, we're gonna
  have a party
Meet me at Mary's place, we're gonna
  have a party
Tell me how do you live broken-hearted
Meet me at Mary's place

I got a picture of you in my locket
I keep it close to my heart
It's a light shining in my breast
Leading me through the dark
Seven days, seven candles
In my window lighting your way
Your favorite record's on the turntable
I drop the needle and pray (Turn it up)
Band's countin' out midnight (Turn it
  up)
Floor's rumblin' loud (Turn it up)

Singer's callin' up daylight (Turn it up)
And waitin' for that shout from the
  crowd (Turn it up)
Waitin' for that shout from the crowd
  (Turn it up)

Waitin' for that shout from the crowd
  (Turn it up)
Waitin' for that shout from the crowd
  (Turn it up)
Waitin' for that shout from the crowd
  (Turn it up)
Waitin' for that shout from the crowd

Turn it up, turn it up, turn it up
Turn it up, turn it up, turn it up, turn it
  up

Meet me at Mary's place, we're gonna
  have a party
Meet me at Mary's place, we're gonna
  have a party
Tell me how do we get this thing started
Meet me at Mary's place . . .

Let it rain, let it rain, let it rain, let it rain,
  let it rain

paradise

Where the river runs to black
I take the schoolbooks from your pack
Plastics, wire and your kiss
The breath of eternity on your lips

In the crowded marketplace
I drift from face to face
I hold my breath and close my eyes
I hold my breath and close my eyes
And I wait for paradise
And I wait for paradise

The Virginia hills have gone to brown
Another day, another sun goin' down
I visit you in another dream
I visit you in another dream

I reach and feel your hair
Your smell lingers in the air

I brush your cheek with my fingertips
I taste the void upon your lips
And I wait for paradise
And I wait for paradise

I search for you on the other side
Where the river runs clean and wide
Up to my heart the waters rise
Up to my heart the waters rise

I sink 'neath the water cool and clear
Drifting down, I disappear
I see you on the other side
I search for the peace in your eyes
But they're as empty as paradise
They're as empty as paradise

I break above the waves
I feel the sun upon my face

my city of ruins

There's a blood red circle
On the cold dark ground
And the rain is falling down
The church door's thrown open
I can hear the organ's song
But the congregation's gone
My city of ruins
My city of ruins

Now the sweet bells of mercy
Drift through the evening trees
Young men on the corner
Like scattered leaves,
The boarded up windows,
The empty streets
While my brother's down on his knees
My city of ruins
My city of ruins

Come on, rise up! Come on, rise up!
Come on, rise up! Come on, rise up!
Come on, rise up! Come on, rise up!

Come on, rise up! Come on, rise up!

Now there's tears on the pillow
Darlin' where we slept
And you took my heart when you left
Without your sweet kiss
My soul is lost, my friend
Tell me how do I begin again?
My city's in ruins
My city's in ruins

Now with these hands,
With these hands,
With these hands,
With these hands,
I pray Lord
With these hands,
With these hands,
I pray for the strength, Lord
With these hands,
With these hands,
I pray for the faith, Lord

With these hands,
With these hands,
I pray for your love, Lord
With these hands,
With these hands,
I pray for the strength, Lord
With these hands,
With these hands,
I pray for your love, Lord
With these hands,
With these hands,

I pray for your faith, Lord
With these hands,
With these hands,
I pray for the strength, Lord
With these hands,
With these hands

Come on, rise up
Come on, rise up

acknowledgments

'd like to thank all those who worked alongside me in bringing my songs to life, particularily Jon Landau, my good friend and longtime working partner, with whom over the years I've discussed many of the issues and ideas that mattered to me and became central to my work; members of the E Street Band—Roy Bittan, Ernest Carter, Clarence Clemons, Danny Federici, Nils Lofgren, Vini Lopez, David Sancious, Patti Scialfa, Garry Tallent, Steve Van Zandt, and Max Weinberg—whose contributions and performance of my music expanded its boundaries and power; and all the other musicians whose efforts graced my work. I'd also like to thank Chuck Plotkin and Toby Scott for shepherding my songs through the recording process; and Barbara Carr and everyone at Landau Management. Thanks also to our publisher, Avon Books, especially Lou Aronica; David Gorman

330

and his talented production team; and Ann Marie Spagnuolo.

The idea for this book began with Sandy Choron. Her dedication and resilience, as well as that of Harry Choron, through its many incarnations is greatly appreciated. I'd like to thank Bob Santelli for the time we spent together shaping the short pieces that preface each album section. His hard work and companionship made a difficult process enjoyable.

Finally, I'd like to thank my family for their love and patience, and the fans for taking my songs into their lives and making them theirs.

index of song titles

index of first lines

credits

photographs

Mary Alfieri: xii, 20, 24, 36-37
Edie Bascom: 102
Joel Bernstein: 97, 99, 114-15, 120-21, 160-161
Phil Ceccola: 23, 27, 28
Danny Clinch: 294, 296, 298, 300, 302, 303, 304, 307, 313, 325, 326
Peter Cunningham: 13, 26
Matt DiLea: ii
Tony DiLea: 243, 253
David Gahr: 22
Lynn Goldsmith: 163, 165
Todd Kaplan: 202
David Kennedy: 132, 134, 135, 142, 147, 150-51, 175
Annie Leibovitz: 168, 178-79, 186, 188, 192, 208-09, 225, 244-45, 308, 316-317
Fred Lombardi: 4, 8
Jim Marchese: 94, 96, 111, 122, 129, 162, 166
Eric Meola: 40-41
Hart Perry: 6
Neal Preston: 214, 272, 292, 320
Barbara Pyle: 43, 45, 47, 48, 53, 56-57, 60, 65
Herb Ritts: 234
David Rose: 219, 238, 258, 260, 261, 269, 273, 275
Adele Springsteen: 2
Bruce Springsteen, 3
Pam Springsteen: 189, 190, 201, 205, 217, 220, 240, 250-51, 256, 270, 278, 285, 289, 331
Frank Stefanko: 62, 64, 67, 68, 72-73, 92, 156-57
Timothy White: 212, 215

songs

"Blinded by the Light" ©1972 Bruce Springsteen (ASCAP)
"Growin' Up" ©1972 Bruce Springsteen (ASCAP)
"Mary Queen of Arkansas" ©1972 Bruce Springsteen (ASCAP)
"Does This Bus Stop at 82nd Street?" ©1972 Bruce Springsteen (ASCAP)
"Lost in the Flood" ©1972 Bruce Springsteen (ASCAP)
"The Angel" ©1972 Bruce Springsteen (ASCAP)
"For You" ©1972 Bruce Springsteen (ASCAP)
"Spirit in the Night" ©1972 Bruce Springsteen (ASCAP)
"It's Hard to Be a Saint in the City" ©1972 Bruce Springsteen (ASCAP)
"The E Street Shuffle" ©1973 Bruce Springsteen (ASCAP)
"4th of July, Asbury Park (Sandy)" ©1973 Bruce Springsteen (ASCAP)
"Kitty's Back" ©1973 Bruce Springsteen (ASCAP)
"Wild Billy's Circus Story" ©1973 Bruce Springsteen (ASCAP)
"Incident on 57th Street" ©1973 Bruce Springsteen (ASCAP)
"Rosalita (Come Out Tonight)" ©1973 Bruce Springsteen (ASCAP)
"New York City Serenade" ©1973 Bruce Springsteen (ASCAP)
"Thunder Road" ©1975 Bruce Springsteen (ASCAP)
"Tenth Avenue Freeze-out" ©1975 Bruce Springsteen
"Night" ©1975 Bruce Springsteen (ASCAP)
"Backstreets" ©1975 Bruce Springsteen (ASCAP)
"Born to Run" ©1975 Bruce Springsteen (ASCAP)
"She's the One" ©1975 Bruce Springsteen (ASCAP)
"Meeting Across the River" ©1975 Bruce Springsteen (ASCAP)
"Jungleland" ©1975 Bruce Springsteen (ASCAP)
"Badlands" ©1978 Bruce Springsteen (ASCAP)
"Adam Raised a Cain" ©1978 Bruce Springsteen (ASCAP)
"Something in the Night" ©1978 Bruce Springsteen (ASCAP)
"Candy's Room" ©1978 Bruce Springsteen (ASCAP)
"Racing in the Street" ©1978 Bruce Springsteen (ASCAP)
"The Promised Land" ©1978 Bruce Springsteen (ASCAP)
"Factory" ©1978 Bruce Springsteen (ASCAP)
"Streets of Fire" ©1978 Bruce Springsteen (ASCAP)
"Prove It All Night" ©1978 Bruce Springsteen (ASCAP)
"Darkness on the Edge of Town" ©1978 Bruce Springsteen (ASCAP)
"The Ties That Bind" ©1980 Bruce Springsteen (ASCAP)
"Sherry Darling" ©1980 Bruce Springsteen (ASCAP)
"Jackson Cage" ©1980 Bruce Springsteen (ASCAP)
"Two Hearts" ©1980 Bruce Springsteen (ASCAP)
"Independence Day" ©1980 Bruce Springsteen (ASCAP)
"Hungry Heart" ©1980 Bruce Springsteen (ASCAP)
"Out in the Street" ©1980 Bruce Springsteen (ASCAP)
"Crush on You" ©1980 Bruce Springsteen (ASCAP)
"You Can Look (But You Better Not Touch)" ©1980 Bruce Springsteen (ASCAP)
"I Wanna Marry You" ©1980 Bruce Springsteen (ASCAP)
"The River" ©1980 Bruce Springsteen (ASCAP)
"Point Blank" ©1980 Bruce Springsteen (ASCAP)
"Cadillac Ranch" ©1980 Bruce Springsteen (ASCAP)
"I'm a Rocker" ©1980 Bruce Springsteen (ASCAP)
"Fade Away" ©1980 Bruce Springsteen (ASCAP)
"Stolen Car" ©1980 Bruce Springsteen (ASCAP)
"Ramrod" ©1980 Bruce Springsteen (ASCAP)
"The Price You Pay" ©1980 Bruce Springsteen (ASCAP)
"Drive All Night" ©1980 Bruce Springsteen (ASCAP)
"Wreck on the Highway" ©1980 Bruce Springsteen (ASCAP)
"Nebraska" ©1982 Bruce Springsteen (ASCAP)
"Atlantic City" ©1982 Bruce Springsteen (ASCAP)
"Mansion on the Hill" ©1982 Bruce Springsteen (ASCAP)
"Johnny 99" ©1982 Bruce Springsteen (ASCAP)
"Highway Patrolman" ©1982 Bruce Springsteen (ASCAP)
"State Trooper" ©1982 Bruce Springsteen (ASCAP)
"Used Cars" ©1982 Bruce Springsteen (ASCAP)
"Open All Night" ©1982 Bruce Springsteen (ASCAP)
"My Father's House" ©1982 Bruce Springsteen (ASCAP)
"Reason to Believe" ©1982 Bruce Springsteen (ASCAP)
"Born in the U.S.A." ©1984 Bruce Springsteen (ASCAP)
"Cover Me" ©1982 Bruce Springsteen (ASCAP)
"Darlington County" ©1984 Bruce Springsteen (ASCAP)
"Working on the Highway" ©1984 Bruce Springsteen (ASCAP)
"Downbound Train" ©1984 Bruce Springsteen (ASCAP)
"I'm on Fire" ©1984 Bruce Springsteen (ASCAP)
"No Surrender" ©1984 Bruce Springsteen (ASCAP)
"Bobby Jean" ©1984 Bruce Springsteen (ASCAP)
"I'm Goin' Down" ©1984 Bruce Springsteen (ASCAP)

"Glory Days" ©1984 Bruce Springsteen (ASCAP)
"Dancing in the Dark" ©1984 Bruce Springsteen (ASCAP)
"My Hometown" ©1984 Bruce Springsteen (ASCAP)
"Ain't Got You" ©1987 Bruce Springsteen (ASCAP)
"Tougher Than the Rest" ©1987 Bruce Springsteen (ASCAP)
"All That Heaven Will Allow" ©1987 Bruce Springsteen (ASCAP)
"Spare Parts" ©1987 Bruce Springsteen (ASCAP)
"Cautious Man" ©1987 Bruce Springsteen (ASCAP)
"Walk Like a Man" ©1987 Bruce Springsteen (ASCAP)
"Tunnel of Love" ©1987 Bruce Springsteen (ASCAP)
"Two Faces" ©1987 Bruce Springsteen (ASCAP)
"Brilliant Disguise" ©1987 Bruce Springsteen (ASCAP)
"One Step Up" ©1987 Bruce Springsteen (ASCAP)
"When You're Alone" ©1987 Bruce Springsteen (ASCAP)
"Valentine's Day" ©1987 Bruce Springsteen (ASCAP)
"Human Touch" ©1992 Bruce Springsteen (ASCAP)
"Soul Driver" ©1992 Bruce Springsteen (ASCAP)
"57 Channels (And Nothin' On)" ©1992 Bruce Springsteen (ASCAP)
"Cross My Heart" ©1992 Bruce Springsteen (ASCAP) and Sonny Boy
   Williamson/ARC Music (BMI)
"Gloria's Eyes" ©1992 Bruce Springsteen (ASCAP)
"With Every Wish" ©1992 Bruce Springsteen (ASCAP)
"Roll of the Dice" ©1992 Bruce Springsteen (ASCAP)
"Real World" ©1992 Bruce Springsteen (ASCAP)
"All or Nothin' At All" ©1992 Bruce Springsteen (ASCAP)
"Man's Job" ©1992 Bruce Springsteen (ASCAP)
"I Wish I Were Blind" ©1992 Bruce Springsteen (ASCAP)
"The Long Goodbye" ©1992 Bruce Springsteen (ASCAP)
"Real Man" ©1992 Bruce Springsteen (ASCAP)
"Better Days" ©1992 Bruce Springsteen (ASCAP)
"Lucky Town" ©1992 Bruce Springsteen (ASCAP)
"Local Hero" ©1992 Bruce Springsteen (ASCAP)
"If I Should Fall Behind" ©1992 Bruce Springsteen (ASCAP)
"Leap of Faith" ©1992 Bruce Springsteen (ASCAP)
"The Big Muddy" ©1992 Bruce Springsteen (ASCAP)
"Living Proof" ©1992 Bruce Springsteen (ASCAP)
"Book of Dreams" ©1992 Bruce Springsteen (ASCAP)
"Souls of the Departed" ©1992 Bruce Springsteen (ASCAP)
"My Beautiful Reward" ©1992 Bruce Springsteen (ASCAP)
"The Ghost of Tom Joad" ©1995 Bruce Springsteen (ASCAP)
"Straight Time" ©1995 Bruce Springsteen (ASCAP)
"Highway 29" ©1995 Bruce Springsteen (ASCAP)
"Youngstown" ©1995 Bruce Springsteen (ASCAP)
"Sinaloa Cowboys" ©1995 Bruce Springsteen (ASCAP)
"The Line" ©1995 Bruce Springsteen (ASCAP)
"Balboa Park" ©1995 Bruce Springsteen (ASCAP)
"Dry Lightning" ©1995 Bruce Springsteen (ASCAP)
"The New Timer" ©1995 Bruce Springsteen (ASCAP)
"Across the Border" ©1995 Bruce Springsteen (ASCAP)
"Galveston Bay" ©1995 Bruce Springsteen (ASCAP)
"My Best Was Never Good Enough" ©1995 Bruce Springsteen (ASCAP)
"Streets of Philadelphia" © 1993 Bruce Springsteen (ASCAP)
"Secret Garden" © 1995 Bruce Springsteen (ASCAP)
"Murder Incorporated" © 1995 Bruce Springsteen (ASCAP)
"Blood Brothers" © 1995 Bruce Springsteen (ASCAP)
"This Hard Land" © 1995 Bruce Springsteen (ASCAP)
"Land of Hope and Dreams" © 2001 Bruce Springsteen (ASCAP)
"American Skin (41 Shots)" © 2001 Bruce Springsteen (ASCAP)
"Lonesome Day" © 2002 Bruce Springsteen (ASCAP)
"Into the Fire" © 2002 Bruce Springsteen (ASCAP)
"Waitin' On a Sunny Day" © 2002 Bruce Springsteen (ASCAP)
"Nothing Man" © 2002 Bruce Springsteen (ASCAP)
"Countin' On a Miracle" © 2002 Bruce Springsteen (ASCAP)
"Empty Sky" © 2002 Bruce Springsteen (ASCAP)
"Worlds Apart" © 2002 Bruce Springsteen (ASCAP)
"Let's Be Friends (Skin to Skin)" © 2002 Bruce Springsteen (ASCAP)
"Further On (Up the Road)" © 2002 Bruce Springsteen (ASCAP)
"The Fuse" © 2002 Bruce Springsteen (ASCAP)
"Mary's Place" © 2002 Bruce Springsteen (ASCAP)
"You're Missing" © 2002 Bruce Springsteen (ASCAP)
"The Rising" © 2002 Bruce Springsteen (ASCAP)
"Paradise" © 2002 Bruce Springsteen (ASCAP)
"My City of Ruins" © 2002 Bruce Springsteen (ASCAP)